LOVE IN YOUR LIFE

$\mathcal{L}$OVE *in* $\mathcal{Y}$our $\mathcal{L}$IFE

A JEWISH VIEW OF TEENAGE SEXUALITY

Roland B. Gittelsohn

UAHC Press
New York, New York

Library of Congress Cataloging-in-Publication Data

Gittelsohn, Roland Bertram, 1910-

  Love in your life: a Jewish view of teenage sexuality/by Roland B. Gittelsohn.

    p. cm.

  Includes bibliographical references.

  Summary: Provides a Jewish perspective on issues concerning
teenage sexuality in the 1990s.

  ISBN 0-8074-0460-8: $9.95

  1. Sexual ethics for teenagers–Juvenile literature.

  2. Sex-Religious aspects–Judaism–Juvenile literature.

  [1. Sex instruction for youth. 2. Sexual ethics. 3. Judaism.] I. Title.

HQ35. G49 1991   90-27689

296.3'8566–dc20   CIP

                                           AC

PHOTOGRAPHS BY JOY WEINBERG

THIS BOOK IS PRINTED ON RECYCLED PAPER

10 9 8 7 6 5 4 3 2 1

Publication of this book was made possible
by a generous grant from the
AUDRE AND BERNARD RAPOPORT
Library Fund

To the many hundreds of young people
at Temple Israel of Boston,
who encouraged and enheartened me through the years
as we talked together about the values of Judaism
and modern science concerning love,
sexuality, and marriage.

MY FERVENT GRATITUDE

To Rabbi Daniel B. Syme and Dr. Sol Gordon, who originally suggested a need for this book and encouraged me to postpone other projects in its favor.

To Aron Hirt-Manheimer and Stuart Benick for their scrupulous attention to editorial and publication details.

To Joy Weinberg for supplying the photographs that enhance my words.

ROLAND B. GITTELSOHN
Boston, Massachusetts
May 1991

CONTENTS

FOREWORD

For more than five decades, the career of Rabbi Roland B. Gittelsohn has embodied courage, compassion, and leadership.

As the Jewish chaplain of the Fifth Marine Division at Iwo Jima in World War II, he delivered a sermon at the dedication of the division cemetery. As a distinguished congregational rabbi, as president of the Central Conference of American Rabbis, as founding president of the Association of Reform Zionists of America, and as chairman of the Reform movement's Commission on Jewish Education, Rabbi Gittelsohn has compiled an unparalleled record of service to Jews and to Judaism.

With this volume, *Love in Your Life: A Jewish View of Teenage Sexuality,* Roland Gittelsohn again demonstrates his vision and his willingness to take on tough issues of concern to young people and adults alike. Close to three decades ago, he first affirmed the then controversial notion that Jewish education must include frank and open discussion of human sexuality in the context of Jewish values. Today, especially in light of the AIDS epidemic and the burgeoning rates of divorce and family disintegration, his pioneering vision has become conventional wisdom.

This book contains the concentrated insights of many decades of study and experience. No subject is taboo. No human situation is too controversial. Roland Gittelsohn does not "play it safe." As a result, readers will confront reality without any of the all-too-common cosmeticizing of language and avoidance of painful issues.

This book may surprise you with its candor. If you read and study it with care, however, it may also change your life. I commend it to you and know that it will be a staple in Jewish education for many years to come.

DANIEL B. SYME
Vice-President
Union of American Hebrew Congregations

WHAT WOULD YOU DO?

*M*AKING OUT Joe and Lois, both high school seniors, have been dating steadily now for nearly two years. Each feels a strong sexual attraction for the other, so much so that when they are alone together they find it difficult to control themselves. On their last few dates Joe has tried to persuade Lois to have intercourse. She feels torn between strong sexual excitement when she is with Joe and an equally strong sense that it would be wrong to go all the way.

"Look, Lois," Joe has said several times, "it just isn't fair for us to get so aroused, only to stop before the tension is released. We're probably the only couple we know who date only each other and haven't done it. If you really love me as you say you do, you'll say yes. If you keep refusing, it makes me wonder whether you really love me."

If you were Lois, how would you respond? Here are several answers she might give:

"I think you're right, Joe. It isn't as if we had just started dating. Our feelings for each other have passed the test of time; I owe it to you to drop my resistance. I'm ready for more if you are."

"Joe, please don't force me to do something that will make me feel guilt the rest of my life."

"If you really love me, Joe, you won't ask me to do something when I'm not ready. I don't think a couple should have sex until they know for sure they are in love and intend to marry. Despite our strong feelings for each other, we're not really old enough yet to know whether this is love or just strong infatuation. I'll be more comfortable if we wait."

"I agree with you, Joe: it's getting harder and harder to stop without going all the way. So maybe we'd better limit ourselves to just a good-night kiss."

If you were Lois, which of these do you think would be your best response? Can you think of others that would be even better? If you were Joe, what would your reaction be to each of these suggestions? How old do you think a person should be before having intercourse? On what conditions and at what time in their relationship should a couple begin to experience intercourse?

*B*I... Sometime after their engagement had been announced, Ed told Carla he was bisexual. He had enjoyed intercourse both with females and on a few occasions with other males, though, since they started dating , he had felt less attracted to males. Naturally this revelation had upset Carla enormously, so much so that her first inclination had been to break the engagement.

"Please don't do that," Ed had protested. "Why should you punish me for being honest? Would you have preferred my keeping this information to myself, marrying you without telling you the truth? I'm sure our love is strong enough to overcome whatever homosexual inclinations I may have had. If I can satisfy my sexual needs with you, I won't need to explore with others, either female or male."

What would you do or say if you were Carla? Should Ed's confession worry her any more than if he had admitted having "affairs" with a number of young women? Should Carla accept Ed's assurances? Should she feel he has done something immoral or abnormal? Do you think Ed will be happy if he and Carla marry?

*P*ERSON OR SOCCER BALL? Sue was four years old when her parents were divorced. At times during the eleven years since then she has felt like a soccer ball, being kicked back and forth by opposing teams. The bitterness attending her parents' divorce has scarcely diminished with time. They still resent each other very much; each says nasty things about the other to

Sue, acting as if each were competing for her loyalty and love.

The fact that they were awarded joint custody by the divorce court adds to Sue's discomfort. She spends half her time with each of them and is really comfortable with neither.

Because, so far as she has been able to tell, her parents' marital discord seems to have arisen mostly after her birth, Sue feels partly responsible for the failure of their marriage. She still has occasional dreams where she either dies or disappears, after which her parents reunite.

Recently Sue's mother has started dating a man Sue doesn't like. She cringes whenever he's in the house, feeling especially uncomfortable on the rare occasions when he stays overnight. Without actually verbalizing it, she has the impression that he is trying to usurp her father's place in the family. She also resents the fact that her mother seems to be flouting the strict code of sexual ethics Sue herself is expected to follow.

Is Sue realistic in feeling guilty over the failure of her parents' marriage? Whose side should she take in their dispute? How do you think she should behave when either parent criticizes the other in her presence? Is she being fair to her mother in reacting as she has to her new dating partner? What can either parent do to make Sue feel more comfortable? What effect, if any, do you think Sue's experiences are likely to have on her own eventual marriage?

*S*ELF-CENTERED? As far back as he can remember, Martin has masturbated several times a week. When he does this, he usually fantasizes that he is having sex with an attractive girl or woman. When his mother first caught him masturbating at age seven, she was appalled. She warned him that he was committing a very serious sin, one that could cause him to suffer from any number of afflictions, including blindness, and that might prevent him from ever having a normal adult sex life. She so frightened him that he vowed to stop. Though this promise has been repeated many times in the ensuing nine years, he has never been able to keep it. He feels increasingly guilty over his "addiction" to what his mother describes as his "nasty habit." He is reluctant to discuss the matter with any of his friends, worried that he may well be the only one among them who masturbates.

Has Martin's mother done her best to help him? Is there any-thing else she could or should do? Is Martin wise in failing to heed her warnings? In keeping this behavior to himself? Is he committing a sin? Will he outgrow the need to masturbate after beginning to have sexual intercourse? Who might best be able to help him? His physician? Rabbi? Camp counselor? A trusted teacher? One of his peers?

A SAMPLING The above scenarios illustrate some of the problems we shall be considering throughout this book. In the chapters that follow, we shall also contemplate such matters as: how to tell whether you're really in love, the relationship and differ-ence between love and sex, dating, whether to have premarital sex, some of what Judaism teaches about sex and marriage, how to choose a mate, information about AIDS and other sexually transmit-ted diseases, and homosexuality, among others.

B EGINNINGS Your sexual education began long before you were even aware of it. When your mother first held you in her arms as an infant, you were learning something about love and the pleasures physical contact could bring to people who love each other. When you observed from earliest childhood how your parents interacted in your home, you were learning many things about being in a relationship. When you first discovered that certain parts of your body were more sensitive and pleasurable to the touch than others, you were beginning to learn important lessons about sex. Your education in this area has been accruing since the moment of your birth.

Unfortunately not all of it has been positive. Your parents and teachers may have been reluctant to transmit the information and attitudes you need; you may thus have been forced to obtain at least some of your information from friends, never fully knowing whether or not that information is accurate. Of the men and women who responded to the famous Kinsey Report, only 5 percent cited their parents as the principal source of their information on sex; in fact, studies indicated that no more than 30 to 40 percent of high school youths received most of their sex education from their parents.

A majority of both boys and girls had received most of their sex facts from peers. Unfortunately, too often such "education" amounts to little more than the blind leading the blind. When college freshmen were asked which topics they found most difficult to discuss with their parents, 85 percent answered sex; almost as many listed love, courtship, and marriage. Between a third and a half admitted that most of their information in these areas had come from friends. Intelligent judgments are possible concerning both marriage and the sex decisions you face now only when based on accurate knowledge and sound advice.

One perceptive observer with a sense of humor has commented: "Considering the way most of us learned about sex, it's a wonder we can do it, do it well, or have any interest in doing it at all."[1]

If you are among the fortunate few whose parents have felt comfortable enough about family and sex to discuss these subjects with you fully and freely, you have a head start. It is possible though that there are areas not covered, misconceptions awaiting correction, and questions that remain unanswered. Some parents, much as they would like to help their sons and daughters, find themselves unable to do so because they themselves were not adequately informed in their own youth.

A further reason why this is precisely the time of life when questions of love, sex, and marriage must be faced is because it is during the high school and early college years that most young people begin to feel a host of sensations, desires, needs, and fears arising from their sexual development. Even for those who postpone any serious thought of marriage until later, evidence attests that very few people later change the type of sex behavior they establish for themselves at this stage of their lives. The kind of relationship you develop now with sexual partners, your dating habits, your attitudes and conduct with regard to sex, all have a direct bearing on the success of your marriage. In short, enough is at stake in terms of your present needs and doubts as well as your eventual marital happiness to make the concerns of this book among the most important you face.

*W*HAT DO YOU THINK? This year for the first time Sarah's school is offering an elective course in sex education. While she herself is most eager to enroll, her parents have decided to exercise their right to refuse permission. They argue there is already too much emphasis on sex in our society, and the course will increase the students' sexual curiosity and desire.

The proper place for sex education, says Sarah's parents, is the home not school. When the time comes for Sarah to be married, her husband will be able to teach her about sex; she doesn't need that information now in her junior year of high school.

With whom do you side, Sarah or her parents? Why? How valid is her parents' view that home is the best place for sex education? Their insistence that Sarah doesn't need this information yet? That her husband can provide it at the proper time?

How adequate has your sex education been? Has it been provided mostly by your parents? Peers? School? Religious education? Books? Newspapers and magazine articles? With whom do you now feel free to discuss your sexual questions and problems? On whom can you depend for accurate and sound advice?

NOTES
WHAT WOULD YOU DO?
  1. C. L. Mithers, in *Glamour*, March 1987.

ARE YOU NOW OR HAVE YOU EVER BEEN IN LOVE?

Donald and Jo are so "madly in love" they can scarcely bear being apart. All day long on the job he thinks of her and can barely wait for the evening when they can be together again. They used to date with one or two other couples but recently are spending their evenings more and more alone. Other people just seem to distract their attention, delaying the hour they really desire—the time when they can curl up together in the comfortable living room chair. Their mutual attraction has become stronger and stronger in the six months since their meeting, convincing them both that their love is genuine. They have had intercourse, which they find mutually exciting and pleasurable.

Is this a case of love or infatuation? How significant is it that they have felt this way for six months and that their feelings toward each other grow stronger and stronger? Would their situation be improved if they were able to marry now?

Jo's favorite leisure-time activities are reading and attending classical music concerts. Don is a sports fanatic; when he isn't playing tennis or basketball himself, he's glued to athletic events on television.

They argue a great deal. Since Don is more dominant, he nearly always prevails when they disagree.

Do you think Don and Jo are in love? What's good about their relationship? Not so good? How important is their mutual sexual pleasure in determining whether or not they are really in love? If they marry, how successful do you think their marriage will be?

Now write down your own definition of love. Later you can compare it to mine.

*M*ANY LOVES *"I love my school, I love my wife, I love oranges, I love my brother..."* You have probably heard each of these statements, though in each the word *love* is obviously used in quite a different sense. This illustrates how many varied connotations the word has and how very difficult it is to define. For our purpose, we are interested chiefly in one special kind of love: the love uniting two individuals in what they expect will be a permanent partnership that includes a sexual relationship. This kind of love certainly is closely connected with other kinds. Even when we limit ourselves to the kind of love that usually results in marriage, a definition is difficult.

Many attempts have been made. Here are a few:

1. Love is an itchy feeling around the heart that you can't scratch.
2. Love is when each person is more concerned for the other than for himself or herself.
3. If you feel yourself to be in love, you are.
4. Love is the will to extend one's self for the purpose of nurturing one's own or another's spiritual growth.
5. Love is a feeling of tenderness and devotion toward someone, so profound that to share that individual's joys, anticipations, sorrows, and pain is the very essence of living.

*L*OVE OR INFATUATION? You know the usual Hollywood pattern: gorgeous, glamorous woman meets handsome, heroic man, they dance to soft music under the stars, know at once that each is meant for the other, it's love at first sight, and they live happily ever after. . . . Or do they? That depends on whether the question applies to an imaginary role or the real life of the movie stars, so many of whose marriages fail.

This Hollywood myth can become frustrating and dangerous because, for a young person especially, it is so very difficult to distinguish among love, infatuation, and romance; the early manifestations and sensations of all three are exasperatingly similar. Probably whatever strong emotional bonds a teenager has felt toward a contemporary of the opposite sex have been infatuation rather than love.

Because far too many couples fail to distinguish between the two feelings in time to avert disappointment and tragedy, it is vital for us to think about the differences. There are primarily four:

1. The first gauge is the test of time. Love has an enduring quality that infatuation lacks. Infatuation is like a match igniting a pile of combustible brush. The flame catches at once, bursts immediately into a frightening fullness that gives the appearance of lasting forever, then quickly subsides and dies. Love is more like a fire built from small beginnings–first, a few pieces of kindling, then larger logs to build the flame, steady replenishment when needed, glowing coals to warm oneself for many hours.

2. A second feature distinguishing infatuation from love is whether the emphasis is on the self or the other person, on getting or giving. Those who are infatuated are really mostly interested in themselves; the objects of their infatuation are important only for what they can provide. The frame of reference is: *how much pleasure it gives me to be with you.* Those who are truly in love are at least as interested in their mate as in themselves; they become more important to themselves in proportion to what they are able to give or to do for their mate. In true love the frame of reference is: *how much more adequate and secure each of us feels because of the other.*

Dr. Harry Stack Sullivan, a well-known psychoanalyst, has said love begins when one feels another person's needs to be as important as one's own–not *more* important, but *as* important.

3. Couples who are infatuated are interested exclusively in themselves. They prefer to spend most of their time alone. While those who are in love also like to spend some time only in each other's company, they enjoy being with others, too.

4. Finally, infatuation is a purely physical experience, while love is both physical and spiritual. By *spiritual* I mean that two people are together interested in creating or appreciating beauty, in discovering or understanding truth, and in improving themselves ethically. True, infatuation involves emotions, too, but they are less stable and mature than the emotions of love. It is important to note that love is no less physical than infatuation, but where the one is physical *only*, the other is physical *plus*. If the primary or sole interest two people have in each other is physical, if their principal joint activity is sexual, we can be sure it is an instance of infatuation not love. To say that love is a spiritual as well as a physical experience is to say that there is something sacred in the love of two people for each

other. This sacredness is precisely what Judaism has always taught.

*S*WORDS AND BEDS Several fascinating assertions in rabbinic literature bear on this discussion. One is the talmudic statement "When love was strong, we could lie, as it were, on the edge of a sword; but now, when love is diminished, a bed sixty ells wide is not broad enough for us."[1]

What were the rabbis attempting to tell us here? Were they in fact speaking of love or of infatuation? Is it possible for true love to become diminished? What is the relationship between love and hate?

Here are two rabbinic views on the meaning of love that apparently contradict each other:

1. "Love without admonition is not love."[2]
2. "Love is blind to defects."[3]

Which of these statements is more realistic or accurate? Why? Can the two be reconciled?

It is possible to arrange a neat list of the four principal differences between infatuation and love, as we have done in this chapter. To distinguish one from the other in actual experience, however, is far more difficult. The feelings that overwhelm a person who is infatuated and sexually attracted to another are among the most powerful in human experience. They are so strong that it often becomes almost impossible to think clearly or judge objectively. It is easy to believe one is primarily interested in another rather than in oneself, that the emotion one feels is broad enough to encompass many others, and that the relationship is spiritual as well as physical even when none of these suppositions actually is true.

This is why the first test of love–the test of time–is perhaps the most important test of all. Hasty marriages are almost never a good idea. Couples who wait patiently, who give themselves the opportunity to apply the test of time, have a much better chance for marital happiness than those who marry in haste.

A rebellious seventeen-year-old was determined to marry her boyfriend despite the warnings of her parents, who were worried because he was a high school dropout with a minor prison record. She wrote in her diary: "Love can blot out reality."

Do you agree? Why? Can infatuation blot out reality? Can romance?

The story ended like this: The two were married and, after several years of turbulence and two children, were divorced.

The eminent psychoanalyst Erich Fromm suggests that the four elements necessary for genuine love are: care, responsibility, respect, and knowledge.[4]

What does it mean for people to care *for each other? To feel* responsible *for each other? To* respect *each other? To* know *each other? Try to think of a specific person with whom you share these four kinds of relationships. Specifically how does each trait manifest itself in behavior?*

Rabbi Eugene B. Borowitz expresses his understanding of love as follows:

> Our beloved is so concerned with our welfare, he will struggle to provide us with whatever we need or desire. He will do anything to prevent harm from befalling us. More, he cares not only for what we are but for what we yet will be. He recognizes our potential and helps us try to reach it. Love thus validates our existence as nothing else can and, with an unparalleled immediacy, helps turn us into the people we always were meant to be.[5]

Is it possible to be infatuated with two people simultaneously? To love two people at the same time?

A SEED IS NOT A FLOWER There is nothing inherently wrong with either infatuation or romance. Either or both of them can in the course of time blossom into love, may indeed be necessary components of love. But to confuse them with love can be calamitous. It makes no more sense than to assume that seed plus oil equals flower. Or that a gourmet dish can be prepared by combining only the first two of its many requisite ingredients.

In order to further distinguish love from both infatuation and romance, ask yourself:
• Is this the kind of person I would welcome as a friend, with whom I would want to spend a lot of time, even if there were no sexual feelings between us? Is our relationship only physical, or also intellectual and spiritual? Is this a person I would find interesting, with whom I would want to spend a great deal of time, from whose companionship I could learn and grow, even if no sexual attraction were involved?
• Does this person try to dominate me, or encourage me instead to nurture and express my own capacities and views? Does he or she pay major attention to my needs or move mostly to satisfy her or his own? When we disagree on matters of importance, does the same one of us nearly always prevail, or do we quite generally share in making decisions?
• Do I feel that our disagreements represent contests of will, in which there is always a winner and a loser? When he or she prevails, do I feel vanquished or silenced?
• How similar are we intellectually? Are we approximately equal in intelligence and academic ambition? In our career plans?
• How similar are we religiously? I refer here not only to formal religious affiliation but also to how important religious faith and practice are to each of us.

A serious study published in the *Journal of Jewish Communal Service* (Winter 1984) revealed that couples who practice religious rituals regularly are six times less likely to be divorced than those who do not. Similarly those who worship in the synagogue at least once a week experience one-fourth the number of divorces that others do.

M Y DEFINITION Many years ago one of my high school classes helped me work out my own definition of love: "Love is a consuming desire to share one's whole life both physically and spiritually with another. It means sharing each other's sorrows and pains no less than one's pleasures and joys. Love is a relationship in which both partners are able to develop their own abilities and fulfill their own hopes in far greater measure than either could have done alone."

How do you react to this definition? Is it better or worse than those suggested earlier in this chapter? What, if anything, is missing from it? Does it apply to love in general (for your parents, a sibling, your best friend) or specifically to the love of mates for each other? Would it be a more accurate, more precise definition of the love that prevails in a good marriage if the word physical *were changed to* sexual?

Love is largely a matter of right emotional relationships. Perhaps an analogy or two will help. Hydrogen and oxygen must exist in the right relationship to each other in order to form water. If, instead of two hydrogen atoms and one oxygen atom, we had one hydrogen atom and two oxygen atoms, the result would not be water. Similarly the various parts of a watch must be located and operating in the right relationship for one to have a timepiece that functions. If the spring is too large or two small, too strong or too weak, in comparison to the other parts, the watch will not work. If all the parts, though they be of the proper size, are thrown into an envelope but not installed in the right interrelationship, everything physically necessary for a watch will be in the envelope, yet there will be no watch. In each of these analogies the sum total of the parts in right relationship to each other is more than the sum total of unorganized parts.

Water is more than just hydrogen plus oxygen. A watch is more than just the parts of which it consists. And a couple in love becomes more than one plus one. Each becomes a better person because of their loving relationship than either could have become without the other.

According to my definition, do you think your parents are really in love? The parents of your friends? Would you be willing to have a marriage like that of your parents?

OTHER VOICES Through the centuries writers and poets have probably concentrated more attention on love than on any other theme. What, if anything, can we learn about love from each of the following selections? Can you add any other literary expression of love that is especially meaningful to you?

And Isaac went out walking in the field toward evening and, looking up, he saw camels approaching. Raising her eyes, Rebekah saw Isaac. She alighted from the camel and said to the servant, "Who is that man walking in the field toward us?" And the servant said, "That is my master." So she took her veil and covered herself. The servant told Isaac all the things that he had done. Isaac then brought her into the tent of his mother Sarah, and he took Rebekah as his wife. Isaac loved her, and thus found comfort after his mother's death.

Genesis 24:63-69

It's true love because
I put on eyeliner and a concerto and make pungent
   observations about the great issues of the day
Even when there's no one here but him,
And because
I do not resent watching the Green Bay Packers
Even though I am philosophically opposed to football,
And because
When he is late for dinner and I know he must be
   either having an affair or lying dead in the middle of a
      street,
I always hope he's dead.
It's true love because
If he said quit drinking martinis but I kept drinking them
    and
  the next morning I couldn't get out of bed,
He wouldn't tell me he told me,
And because
He is willing to wear unironed undershorts
Out of respect for the fact that I am philosophically
   opposed
  to ironing,
And because
If his mother were drowning and I were drowning and he
   had to
  choose one of us to save,

He says he'd save me.
It's true love because
When he went to San Francisco on business while I
   had to stay home with the painters and the exterminator
   and the baby who was getting the chicken pox,
He understood why I hated him,
And because
When I said that playing the stock market was
   juvenile and irresponsible and then the stock I
   wouldn't let him buy went up twenty-six points,
I understood why he hated me,
And because
Despite cigarette cough, tooth decay, acid indigestion,
   dandruff, and other features of married life that tend
   to dampen the fires of passion,
We still feel something
We can call
True love.

Judith Viorst, "True Love," in It's Hard to Be Hip Over
Thirty and Other Tragedies of Married Life (New York: New
American Library, 1968)

I love you.
Not only for what you are,
But for what I am
When I am with you.

I love you
Not only for what
You have made of yourself,
But for what
You are making of me.

I love you for ignoring the possibilities
Of the fool in me
And for laying firm hold
Of the possibilities for good.

Why do I love you?

I love you
For closing your eyes
To the discords–
And for adding to the music in me
By worshipful listening.

I love you because you
Are helping me to make
Of the lumber of my life
Not a tavern
But a temple:
And out of the words
Of my every day
Not a reproach
But a song.

I love you
Because you have done
More than any creed
To make me happy.

You have done it
Without a word,
Without a touch,
Without a sign.
You have done it
Just by being yourself.

After all
Perhaps that is what
Love means.

Roy Croft, "Why Do I Love You?"

WHAT DO YOU THINK Bill and Frances fell madly in love the very first time they met on a blind date four months ago. They have been together practically every evening since.

Before meeting Bill, Frances enjoyed nothing more than curling up before the fireplace with a good book. She has done little reading recently; Bill prefers to spend their evenings together bowling or dancing, and in order to please him she has raised no serious objection. She feels very safe and secure when with him. He seems to know the right answer whenever she herself is in doubt. He is able and willing to make decisions without troubling her.

Bill remembers that when he was a child his mother, who had to carry most of the family burdens because his father was a weak person, lived an unhappy life. And he does not want his wife to face a similar situation. He feels that a man who truly loves his wife will protect her as far as possible from all difficulty. Because of his strong conviction about this, he makes nearly all the important decisions for the two of them. When they are married, he expects to handle all the details of their budget and checking account, giving Frances a generous allowance and sparing her the trouble of managing any money matters. When he faces business reverses or worries, he does not mention them to her; he wants her to be happy. These are some of the reasons Frances feel confident and secure. She is sure they will have a happy life together.

Would you characterize this relationship as love, romance, or infatuation? Why? Do Frances and Bill seem to meet each other's needs? Does each encourage the other to develop more of his or her potential? How successful do you think their marriage will be?

NOTES
ARE YOU NOW OR HAVE YOU EVER BEEN IN LOVE?
1. *Sanhedrin* 72.
2. *Bereshit Rabbah* 54.
3. *Sanhedrin* 105.
4. Erich Fromm, *The Art of Loving* (New York: Harper & Bros., 1956), p. 26.
5. E. Borowitz, *Choosing a Sex Ethic* (New York: Schocken Books, 1969), p. 73.

THE RIGHT TIME

Rabbi K. was on the spot. Leah and Philip, two of his favorite young congregants, had appealed to him for support. At the ages of eighteen and twenty-one respectively, they wanted very much to marry. Leah was a freshman in college, Philip a senior. They had known each other for five years and had been going steady for over two. As you may already have suspected, their parents were vigorously opposed to their being married. But they had agreed to invite the rabbi for dinner and listen to his advice.

The young couple argued that each set of parents was prepared to continue supporting their son or daughter through graduate study anyway and that with little more than that they could get along all right. The parents expressed great fear that Leah especially wasn't old enough for marriage. They were concerned, moreover, about what would happen if she became pregnant. That might well mean dropping all their study plans and changing the whole course of their lives. When confronted with the very high rate of divorce among those who marry at a young age, Philip and Leah said they were aware of the risks but felt sure they would be among the successful couples; they were confident they loved each other enough to surmount all difficulties and problems.

What advice would you give if you were Rabbi K? Were the parents realistic in fearing the possibility of pregnancy? If Leah did become pregnant and either or both of them had to drop out of school as a consequence, what effect do you think this might have on their marriage? How much weight should be given to the couple's

confidence that they would be different, that they could avoid the risks involved? What problems either than the possibility of pregnancy might they face?

Love demands a high level of maturity. Little children love their parents because all their needs are fulfilled by them: the children don't have to do anything for or give anything to their parents in order to receive love. No marriage can succeed if the partners enter into it on the childish basis of having their needs met by the other, with nothing positive provided in return. To be successful, marriage must involve a mutuality in which both mates not only receive but give love, in which the needs of both are met. Nearly all normal high-school-age young people are capable of experiencing romance and/ or infatuation. Very few have yet achieved a level of maturity that augurs well for real love and marriage.

*P*ROOF OF THE PUDDING How successful are early marriages? The record is not very encouraging. One authority tells us there are six times as many divorces in marriages where both spouses were under twenty-one at the time of their wedding as when both were over thirty-one.[1] Another survey reveals that three of five teenage marriages end in divorce within three years.[2]

Parade Magazine published a survey of several hundred men and women who had graduated from high school six years earlier. Almost half were married, and almost half of these had married before both partners had reached the age of twenty. Regardless of whether or not they were married at the time of the interview, seven out of ten said they were opposed to early marriages. This even included some who reported themselves to be happy in their wedded life. Barbara McIntyre Gross, who had three children and was separated from her husband, said: "At eighteen you're pretty stupid. Maybe I was trying to prove I was grown-up. I thought I knew better than my parents, better than everyone."

Samuel R. Porter who dropped out of college one year after his wedding said: "It's the biggest mistake of my life, and I'll regret it for the rest of my life. We should have waited. When I was eighteen, I wouldn't listen. I'm sorry I didn't."

Not all of those interviewed felt this way. Garlynn Rodriguez, who also became a wife at eighteen, said: "I think that marriage matured me more than anything else. Learning to live with someone else and sharing his life–that makes you grow up much faster."

Two leading experts have summarized their conclusion as follows: "It's our conviction that many persons marry when they are too young, not necessarily in years but in maturity, in experience and in the ability to meet the many responsibilities of family living. Such marriages are 'bad' marriages, not perhaps because the couple is unsuited to each other, not because of any deficiencies in the persons concerned other than those which time can erase, but because they have assumed life's major responsibility before they were ready to do so. It injures a young horse to do heavy work too soon, the best automobile should not be overtaxed when it is new, a plank breaks when it is overloaded. . . . A child should not undertake an adult's job. Marriage means much more than the legality of sharing a common bed."[3]

*T*WO SCENARIOS Often when two individuals unite in marriage while they are both very young and their union seems at first to be successful, in the course of time it fails. This may well be because, though they seemed to be reasonably compatible at the time of their wedding, they subsequently matured at different paces or in divergent directions. As I write these sentences I think of a young woman who married a clergyman when, at age nineteen, she seemed to be well matched with him in both religious inclination and social preference. Upon completion of her graduate studies, however, she developed a taste for an executive career of her own and a social life, which would be quite awkward in connection with her husband's career. The end result was that they were divorced about a dozen years after their marriage.

This young woman's father had urged her, when she was nineteen, to postpone marrying. When she tearfully told him of her divorce plans, she said, "Dad, every word you spoke twelve years ago was 100 percent true!" He then replied to her: "Was there anything I could have said or done then to convince you?" She answered him: "Of course not; I had to learn the hard way." She would no doubt be the first to agree now that it would have spared her, her husband, and their children much pain had she realized the truth earlier.

Not long ago a good friend of mine explained the failure of his first marriage as follows: "When we were married, neither of us knew yet who he or she really was. How could we possibly have known whether we were right for each other?"

No person is a static entity. We change and grow constantly throughout our lives, most notably and dramatically between the ages of puberty and full adulthood. Two individuals who are compatible at age twenty and who grow in the same direction and at pretty much the same pace will be even more compatible at age thirty or forty. If, however, one matures very much faster than the other or in a different direction, an initially minor discrepancy between them can become an unbridgeable gap.

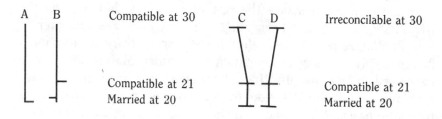

A and B were more fortunate in their marriage than C and D. At the time of their marriage, however, both couples gambled; there was no way then to be sure. All other things being equal, the more each prospective mate knows his or her adult nature and preferences when they are married, the greater will be their chance for happiness together.

WORTH PONDERING *What do you feel is the proper age for love and marriage? Is it the same for everyone? Should marriage or a career come first for boys? For girls? Do you think you yourself are old enough to experience genuine love for someone of the opposite sex who is approximately your own age? Have you ever been in love? What do people often refer to as "puppy love"? How does it differ from real love? Should a couple be financially self-sufficient before they marry? In answering these questions consider the following quotation from rabbinic literature and decide how valid it is for today.*

A man should build himself a home, plant himself a vineyard, and then bring into the home a bride. Fools are they who marry while they have no secure livelihood.

*T*IME FOR A DEFINITION I have stressed the importance of maturity as a requirement for both love and a good marriage. But this will remain only a vague and not very helpful generality unless we explore what the word *maturity* means. Students of human behavior have devoted many hours and innumerable volumes to the subject. Most of them would agree that the following traits distinguish mature people:

1. *Mature people learn from experience and grow as a result of their errors.* Being imperfect human beings, they will probably continue to make mistakes the rest of their lives but will, on the whole, successfully avoid repeating the same ones over and over.

2. *Mature people willingly assume responsibility.* A child must be repeatedly reminded of obligations and duties. Mature adults have developed an inner monitor that tells them these things on their own. Although Judith Viorst speaks from a woman's point of view in the following passage, boys and men should have no difficulty transposing her comments into a male key:

> An adult rinses out her pantyhose and writes thank-you notes even when no one's around to tell her she should. She doesn't spend the gas-bill money on earrings even when no one's around to tell her she shouldn't. A girl relies on other people to define, and remind her of, her obligations, but a grownup has to be her own grownup.
>
> "Judy," my mother would say when I was a teenager, "did you make your bed?"
>
> "Yes, Mom, I did."
>
> "And what about your wastebasket–have you emptied it?"
>
> "Gee, Mom, I can't remember *everything.*"
>
> Now, this little routine isn't strictly the province of eighteen-year-olds. There are thirty-year-olds who want somebody else taking charge. Indeed, with a cooperative, daddylike husband, a wife can spend her whole lifetime playing child-bride, never having to decide when to put on the roast beef or go to the dentist or blow her nose.
>
> A lot of husbands, however, refuse to cooperate.
>
> Six months after she got married, my friend Allison told me, there was a terrible water leak in her apartment. She rushed next door, phoned her husband, and told him he'd better come running home, right away. "You've got to move the furniture and you've got to call the plumber," she wailed, "or everything will be destroyed!" Her husband's reply was icy and inelegant. "Get your ass back over there and do what has to be done." And that's what being a grownup is all about.[4]

Mature people accept responsibility in another sense, too. When the consequences of their conduct are unpleasant, they accept the blame—without destroying themselves and without requiring a scapegoat.

3. *There is purpose to their lives.* They project important goals for themselves and plan their activities as progressive steps toward the attainment of these goals. Thus they feel fulfilled through growth. They avoid just living each day and making each decision as if it were unrelated to any larger objective.

4. *They learn to live with unhappy situations that they can neither change nor honorably avoid.* Recognizing that life cannot always be exactly the way they want it, they distinguish between those circumstances within their power to improve and those to which they must become reconciled.

*M*ATURITY ALSO MEANS 5. *They accept themselves— their virtues as well as their faults.* Since they do not expect to achieve perfection, they need not castigate themselves for falling short of it. They are able to evaluate realistically both their abilities and their deficiencies, trying to enhance the former and avoiding excessive guilt over the latter. They can accept criticism and disappointment because these are balanced by achievement and success. So long as they have done their best, they do not deem failure a disgrace.

6. *Because they don't expect perfection of themselves, they have no need to demand perfection from others.* This applies especially to their parents. Adolescence can be a time of great turbulence between young people and their parents. You may have heard of the twenty-four-year-old who was amazed at how much his father had learned in the past seven years. It is quite likely that more change had occurred in him than in his parents.

It is common knowledge that some of our faults and a good deal of our emotional distress are due to our parents' mistakes in relating to us when we were very young. One mark of immature people is that even in adulthood they use these parental mistakes—real or imaginary—as an excuse for their own deficiencies. I know people in their sixties and seventies who still do this. Maturity means, among other things, accepting our parents for what they are, forgiving their errors, and attempting to improve ourselves, no matter how much we may have been wronged in the past.

7. *They do not need to dominate or control others.* There is enough satisfaction for them in improving themselves, in exercising their own freedom, so that they gladly extend the same freedom of choice to those whose lives touch theirs.

8. *They are able to defer a pleasure they would like to have now* for the sake of a greater joy that cannot come until later and that depends on renouncing the enjoyment immediately available.

No one is mature in all these respects and under all circumstances. We all sometimes act childishly, immaturely.

The best each of us can hope for is to improve, to exhibit greater maturity in these directions with each passing year. Obviously, the more mature two people are, the greater will be the probability of happiness in their marriage.

$\mathcal{L}$OOKING IN THE MIRROR Using the criteria just suggested, how mature do you judge yourself to be? With a friend who knows you well (perhaps someone you have been dating), use the chart on the facing page and the scale below to rate your maturity. Mark yourselves independently, then compare your ratings.

1. Below average
2. Average
3. Above average
4. Superior

I do not recommend doing this, however unless you can tolerate honest criticism of yourself and your friendship with the other person is strong enough to survive such openness, perhaps even gain from it. Comparing your ratings with those your partner has given you can provide a valuable check on how accurately you have evaluated yourself. It may be helpful for you to keep this chart and use it at some future point with the person whom you are planning to marry.

$\mathcal{E}$N ROUTE TO LOVE Every normal human being is born with the capacity to love and a need for love. We do not achieve the kind of love required for marriage, however, until we have grown successfully through a number of earlier stages. Each stage is typical and adequate at the age when it appears. Each is

MATURITY SCALE				
	MY RATINGS		YOUR RATINGS	
	Of Myself	Of You	Of Yourself	Of Me
1. Learns from experience				
2. Assumes responsibility				
3. Has purpose in life				
4. Accepts the inevitable				
5. Accepts, respects self				
6. Concentrates on the task of the present				
7. No need to dominate				
8. Able to postpone pleasure				
9. Demonstrates spontaneity and humor				
10. Possesses capacity to grow				

dangerous if it persists much beyond its proper time. Here are the levels through which we must grow on the road to mature love.

1. *I Love Myself Only.* Tiny infants are at first aware only of themselves. Their universe extends only as far as their own fingers and toes. Other people gradually become important only insofar as they can satisfy the infant's needs. They want what they want when they want it-or else! This stage shouldn't last beyond the age of two years at most.

2. *I Love My Parents and Siblings.* At a fairly early point in life infants begin to be aware of others as existing in their own right. This process begins with their parents, then extends to sisters and brothers. Mother and father, brother and sister become individuals they are able to love for themselves, not just for what they give them. This is normal up to the age of six or seven and unusual beyond eight.

3. *I Love My Gang, Too.* Somewhere along the line children reach out for meaningful relationships that go beyond their own home. They become part of a group, usually made up of others who are their own age and sex. At this point in their lives they are likely to evidence strong antipathy to members of the opposite sex. Their personal importance and self-esteem are reinforced by belonging to a group. Such an attitude as this is characteristic of the early teens and seldom lasts beyond eighteen.

4. *I Like Girls/Boys.* The strong aversion to the opposite sex becomes strangely transformed into an equally strong attraction. We suddenly discover that boys or girls aren't really as abominable as we had supposed. Therefore we like the opposite sex quite generally–any and all of them.

5. *I Like One Girl/One Boy.* The general, diffuse attraction for the opposite sex is narrowed down to one particular person at a time. This is the stage of "crushes"–with the object of one's affections probably changing quite frequently.

6. *I Love the Only One.* In due course the field becomes narrowed to one. Having been attracted to all of the opposite sex, then to one at a time, we reach the point of choosing a permanent partner for life.

Each stage is normal and healthy at a given point in our lives and contributes something to the richness of the next. The more fully we experience the earlier levels of love, the readier we are at the proper time to know the meaning of full marital love. The person who has not yet grown through the first five steps is less likely to be ready for marriage. One danger in early marriages is that one or both of the partners may still be in that category. Then trouble is on the horizon.

Most of us never entirely outgrow these earlier stages. From time to time we may be able to detect some trace of an earlier level, usually in something irrational or inappropriate that we have done. This is nothing to worry about if it happens only on rare occasions. If, however, a person's general behavior is arrested on a level that should have been outgrown, considering marriage may be premature.

How much can you remember in your own life of each stage described above? At which level would you place yourself now? Can you give one example how you have said or felt or done something within recent months that indicates a residue from each of the peri-

ods you have already passed? If you are unable to find illustrations from your own recent experience, try to do so from the behavior of your friends.

In Jewish tradition the Bar or Bat Mitzvah ceremony is a formal, public means of recognizing that a young person has reached a significant stage of maturity.

Do you think it's a good idea for the community to encourage such a public ceremony? Should it be retained, discarded, or changed to a different age? Why? Would it be a good idea, if Bar and Bat Mitzvah are continued, to hold the ceremony not at the same age for everyone, but for each child when he or she gives evidence of sufficient maturity? Are we Jews the only ones who have practiced such a ceremony? In what respects was a thirteen-year-old mature several centuries ago? Now? Using the criteria of maturity listed in this chapter, how mature were you on your thirteenth birthday? Now?

*R*EBOUND AND ESCAPE There are two further possibilities to guard against. Frequently the prospect of marriage—consciously or unconsciously—represents an escape hatch from some seemingly intolerable situation. Sometimes it's an unhappy home or unpleasant parental pressure. Or it may be a frustrating job—an inability to decide which of several vocations to follow—or envy of friends who are already married.

Under any of these circumstances marriage can be not only a means of escape but perhaps also a weapon with which to strike back at the offending party. If a young person knows that a parent is strongly opposed to a marriage, what a wonderful opportunity it may be to assert independence, to get back at the parent for all the abuse—real or alleged—suffered at his or her hands. One expert describes what sometimes happens:

How often is this "love," which some feel, merely the desire to get away from a quarrelsome, bickering family, a dominating mother or a tight little office in which one feels stifled? It is understandable that people should strive to get away from that which annoys them, although the basic reasons for the annoyance may be in themselves. When you marry you *assume* responsibilities; you do not *escape* them. A good marriage will mean that life will be much richer and more worthwhile, but it will not be easier. Marriage creates as many problems as it solves. The success of your marriage will depend upon what you are getting into, not what you "get away from."[5]

In this connection it's important to understand that sometimes young people who are suffering from emotional problems look upon marriage as a possible cure. But people who are having difficulty handling themselves and their problems while single will nearly always experience still greater trouble in marriage. The time to straighten oneself out emotionally is before the wedding not afterward. Though it is true that the responsibilities of marriage can sometimes contribute to an individual's maturity, it is even truer that maturity already achieved increases the probability of a happy marriage.

A second related danger is that of falling into a bad marriage "on the rebound." Men and women who have just been rejected by someone to whom they had been engaged or with whom they had a commitment are often ripe for an unfortunate partnership with someone else. It isn't easy to live through such an experience: to lose a relationship on which you have depended can be very damaging to your self-esteem and pride. What could be more natural than wanting to fill the void as speedily as possible? Natural, yes–but, for that very reason, dangerous! Such individuals are apt to be so anxious to compensate for their recent loss that they fail to consider whether the proposed partner is or is not really the right one for a lifelong relationship.

Either of the dangers just described can be formidable, even when the individuals involved are aware of their motivations. What makes them devilishly difficult–at times even cruelly tragic–is the frequency with which the real dynamics of the behavior are unconscious. When this occurs, it is possible to convince oneself that one is genuinely in love, though such may not be the case at all.

Good rules to follow, therefore, are these: (1) When on the rebound, go slowly. Try not to become emotionally involved again too soon; if you find you are, don't rush into a permanent alliance. Give the old, dependable time test a chance to work. (2) If you have been generally unhappy about your relationship with parents or others or yourself, be suspicious of any overwhelming emotional attachment to someone else. Be as sure as you can that you are moving *toward* something desirable, not *away from* something unpleasant.

*N*O GUARANTEE There is no simple or easy answer to the question of who is old enough for love. Marriage is serious adult business demanding emotional maturity, and that maturity is not just a matter of chronological age. One person may be ready for marriage at nineteen, another not ready at thirty-nine. We must all do the most honest, objective job we can of evaluating our personal maturity and judging whether we have successfully emerged from the necessary earlier stages of development. Only then have we the right to give serious consideration to marriage.

*W*HAT DO YOU THINK? Irene was an awkward, rather homely girl who had never been popular with the boys. As a matter of fact, she didn't have many girlfriends either. She had seldom been asked out on dates; this bothered her a great deal. When she did go out, she felt insecure and unsure of herself.

Last summer Tom asked her for a date. It took a lot of courage on his part, for he, too, had experienced difficulty in social adjustment. He hated to ask a girl for a date because every refusal was a bitter pill to swallow. He and Irene seemed to hit it off well from the start. They dated regularly through the summer and fall, and by spring Tom had "popped the question." Irene's parents were delighted at the favorable turn in her life, but they felt at nineteen she wasn't yet ready for marriage. To tell the truth, Irene had some doubts herself, though she wouldn't admit them to anyone else. She was afraid, however, if she turned Tom down, he would stop dating her and she might never have another chance to marry.

How can you explain why these two got along so well as dating partners? Wouldn't that seem to indicate they would probably have a successful marriage? What would your advice to Irene be? To Tom? Were her fears about never having another chance realistic? Is it better for a girl to accept an offer of marriage despite her doubts or to remain unmarried and possibly alone.

NOTES
THE RIGHT TIME
1. J.H.S. Bossard and E.S. Boll, *Why Marriages Go Wrong* (New York: The Ronald Press, 1958), p. 110.
2. *The New York Times*, June 21, 1978.
3. Bossard and Boll, *Why Marriages Go Wrong.* p. 118.
4. *Redbook* magazine, March 1973.
5. S. Duvall, *Before You Marry* (New York: Association Press, 1949), pp. 10ff.

SEX: FICTION AND FACT

Before proceeding with this chapter, on a separate piece of paper mark the following statements True (T) or False (F).

1. It is impossible for a female to become pregnant the first time she has sexual intercourse.

2. Withdrawal of the penis from the vagina before ejaculation is an effective method of contraception (birth control).

3. Science and religion agree that masturbation is morally wrong and physically harmful.

4. Orgasms (coming to climax) in sexual intercourse are less important for females than for males.

5. Homosexuality is immoral.

6. Pregnancy occurs only when both partners in sexual intercourse reach a climax ("come").

7. A male who has had sexual intercourse before marriage makes a better husband than one who has not.

8. A female who has had sexual intercourse before marriage makes a better wife than one who has not.

9. The so-called rhythm method (limiting intercourse to the days of the month when a female is not ovulating and thus cannot become pregnant) provides effective birth control.

10. Young people who are taught about birth control are more likely to have sexual intercourse than those who are not so instructed.

Every one of the statements above is false. If you marked any of them true, your knowledge of sex isn't as adequate as you might have thought. This and the following chapters will show why you were wrong if you thought any of these assertions were true.

*S*EX AND GOD We are about to trace a most thrilling and exciting story. There is much evidence in the universe—in its orderliness and beauty, in the working together of so very many different elements and parts to serve important purposes—to convince us it could not be the result of mere happenstance or coincidence. The fact that scientists can learn enough about the laws of the universe, and can depend upon those laws to operate without deviation (and to permit us to land with precision on the moon a quarter of a million miles away), is surely evidence enough for most of us that some kind of Intelligence or Power is responsible for everything that exists. We call that Intelligence or Power "God."

None of the evidence we find in outer space and on Earth is more wonderfully convincing of this Intelligence than our own bodies. The most highly skilled engineer, using the most ingenious and complicated computer, could not possibly have planned bodies and minds that operate so efficiently and purposefully as ours do. The facts that, regardless of the temperature outside, the internal heat of the human body in normal health always remains within a fraction of a degree of what it should be . . . that no matter how much or how little liquid we drink, the proportion of water in our bodies is maintained at an even level . . . that when we ascend to higher altitudes where less oxygen is available, the red corpuscles in our blood immediately multiply in order to provide enough oxygen to keep us alive . . . that when infection strikes us, our white corpuscles mobilize at once to defend us—these and countless other manifestations of intelligence in the planning and operation of the human body impress us with the Intelligence permeating the entire universe.

Nowhere is this evidence more compellingly and beautifully illustrated than in the sex life of human beings. Millions of details in structure and function have been so designed that it is possible *through one act* for men and women to propagate their species (that is to say, produce offspring), to enjoy both physical and spiritual delight together, to express and simultaneously enrich their love and intimacy, and to establish the foundation for families. In observing the truly amazing phenomena of human sex, you come perhaps as close as you ever will to witnessing how God operates in our lives.

And someday, in experiencing all this with the man or woman you love, you yourself may come closer than in any other way to God.

*S*EX AND MALES A diagram of the male sexual organs appears below. It shows first of all the penis, which serves the double purpose of conveying from inside to outside the body both urine from the bladder and a liquid substance called semen during sexual excitation. The general term for both the male and female sex organs is genitals.

It is one of nature's incredible feats of engineering that the two functions of the penis could be so incompatible as to make one of them impossible. Urine contains a great deal of acid. Spermatozoa (also called sperm)–the microscopic seeds needed to make a female pregnant–cannot live in the presence of acid. If any acid from urine were to be in the urethra (the tube that extends inside the penis) when sperm are flowing through it, they would immediately be killed and pregnancy could never occur. To prevent this, two things take place when a male becomes sexually excited. First, a muscle closes off the bladder so it becomes impossible for a male who is sexually aroused to urinate; second, the prostate gland produces an alkaline

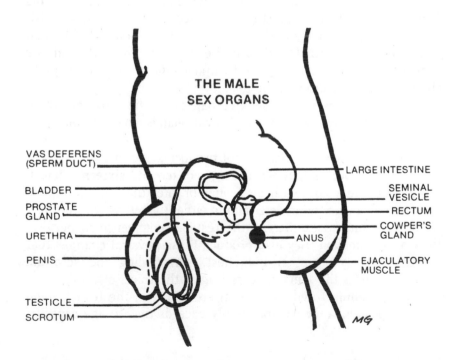

THE MALE
SEX ORGANS

VAS DEFERENS
(SPERM DUCT)

BLADDER

PROSTATE
GLAND

URETHRA

PENIS

TESTICLE

SCROTUM

LARGE INTESTINE

SEMINAL
VESICLE

RECTUM

COWPER'S
GLAND

ANUS

EJACULATORY
MUSCLE

MG

fluid to counteract the effect of any acid that may have remained in the urethra from previous urination, thus enabling the sperm to remain alive.

The size of the penis, like that of all other bodily parts, varies greatly from one person to the next. Normally, when a man is not sexually excited, the penis is in the limp position shown in the diagram and is likely to be about three-and-a-half to four inches in length. When a male is sexually aroused, it projects itself diagonally upward from the body, assuming a probable length of five to six-and-a-half inches. There is no relationship between the size of the penis and the intensity of a male's sexual desires or capacity.

Some males, especially adolescents, are very sensitive about the size of their penises. Though fairly common, this is an unnecessary and unwarranted fear. Like any other part of the body—indeed, like the body as a whole—size is in no way related to function. The important thing for both genders to remember is that your eventual success in a relationship will depend upon who *you* are, the *total you* as a person—not upon the size of your genitals—and that others will be attracted to and will love all of you, not just any one specific part of you.

At birth the tip of the penis is partially covered over with a flap of skin called the foreskin. Circumcision consists of removing this flap so the tip of the penis is fully exposed. Besides being a Jewish religious ritual symbolizing the covenant between God and Abraham, circumcision has been found to be healthier for the male and, for some reason doctors do not yet fully understand, to reduce the probability of uterine cancer in the female.

Beneath the penis is a sack or bag called the scrotum, which contains the testicles, two small oval glands that manufacture sperm.

The testicles are not capable of producing sperm until puberty, which usually occurs between the ages of ten and sixteen. That in some boys it may come a little sooner or later than the average is of no significance at all in determining either the intensity or normality of their future sex life. As the testicles commence to perform their major function they also produce those physical changes that indicate puberty: hair on the chest, surrounding the scrotum, appearing under the arms, a deepening of the voice, etc.

Once manufactured, the sperm are stored in the testicles and the vasa deferentia. When the supply exceeds the storage capacity, they are automatically released in the form of nocturnal emissions or, as they are more commonly called, *wet dreams*. A boy who awakens in the morning to discover that during the night a quantity of liquid was apparently ejected from his penis, perhaps leaving stains on his pajamas and sheet, need not worry; this is nature's perfectly normal way of making room for the storage of more sperm. Often these emissions are accompanied by sexually exciting dreams. These, too, are perfectly normal; they should be the cause of neither fear nor guilt.

Each vas deferens has a seminal vesicle attached to it, the function of which is to supply a yellowish substance that makes the semen thicker, hence better able to carry and preserve the sperm. Ordinarily the seminal vesicles are kept closed by muscles in the prostate gland; it is only during sexual excitement that they open, permitting the secretion to pass into the urethra and become part of the semen.

Finally, there is Cowper's gland—named after the doctor who first discovered it. This gland secretes a slippery fluid that serves the same purpose in sexual intercourse that lubricating oil does in the engine of a car. The upward-downward motion of pistons in their cylinders would create friction that could quickly burn them up if a lubricant were not provided. Similarly the inward-outward motion of the male penis in the female vagina could cause discomfort and pain if adequate lubrication were missing. It is the function of Cowper's gland and of two glands in the female body to furnish such lubrication. The large intestine and anus serve no direct sexual function; they are shown in the diagram just to indicate their relationship to the sex organs.

$\mathcal{S}$EX AND FEMALES

Perhaps even more ingenious than the sexual equipment of males is that of females. It is shown in the next diagram. First there is the vagina, the tube or passage through which sperm enter a female's body; and, if a female becomes pregnant, a fully developed child emerges from her body at the end of nine months. Similar to the male penis, the female vagina varies in size—not only from female to female but in the same female, depending on whether or not she is sexually excited. The vagina expands much more slowly than the penis; but, like the penis, it does enlarge when aroused. The entrance to the vagina is called the vulva.

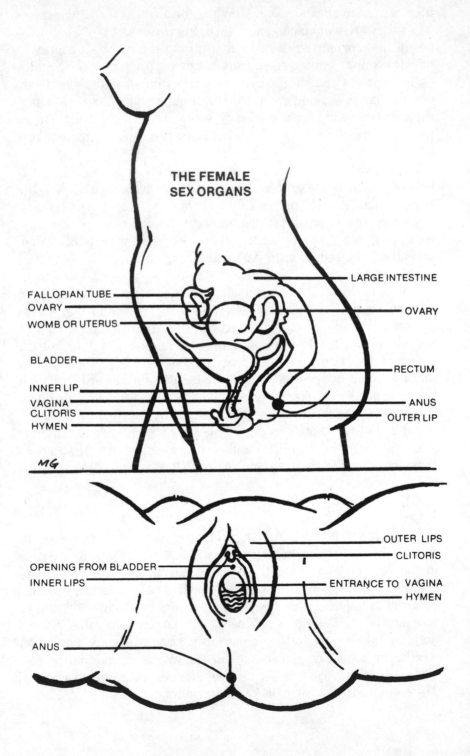

THE FEMALE
SEX ORGANS

FALLOPIAN TUBE
OVARY
WOMB OR UTERUS

BLADDER

INNER LIP
VAGINA
CLITORIS
HYMEN

MG

LARGE INTESTINE

OVARY

RECTUM

ANUS
OUTER LIP

OUTER LIPS
CLITORIS

OPENING FROM BLADDER
INNER LIPS

ENTRANCE TO VAGINA
HYMEN

ANUS

No other part of the body has the automatic elasticity of the female reproductive apparatus. For example, before sexual intercourse has occurred, the opening of the vagina is only about three-fourths of an inch in width; after some months of intercourse it has stretched to approximately an inch and a quarter; during childbirth it expands to five or six inches, then slowly returns to its normal size.

In a female who has never experienced sexual intercourse–the mouth of the vagina is normally covered by a membrane called the hymen. The thickness and toughness of the hymen vary greatly. In many females it becomes so stretched, even before intercourse, as to offer no resistance at all. If the hymen has not been broken or stretched in advance, it may cause slight pain and some bleeding the first time intercourse is experienced; this is nothing to fear. Only in rare instances does the hymen pose a major obstacle to intercourse, and even then medical help can alleviate any serious difficulty.

Ancient peoples believed if the hymen was broken or stretched before a bride's wedding night, this was certain evidence that the bride was not a virgin. In some cultures a white sheet was placed in the marriage bed, and unless it was stained with blood the following morning, the bride was assumed to have had intercourse before and was punished accordingly. While no one in our civilization is quite that crude, there are still some husbands who expect to find an unbroken hymen in their brides. They need to be reminded that the hymen can be stretched in several ways: a broken hymen does not necessarily constitute proof a female is not a virgin.

Near the outer lips of the vagina is an organ called the clitoris. Some theorize it to be a female's vestigial remnant of the male penis. Exactly why females should have this remnant we do not know. Perhaps it is an interesting reminder that in some of the earliest forms of life there was no sharp differentiation between sexes; each organism carried the characteristics and performed the functions of both sexes (androgyny). Only later in evolution did the two sexes become clearly differentiated. In any event, females possess what may be a vestigial penis called the clitoris, while males possess stunted female breasts. The clitoris is the most sexually excitable part of the female anatomy.

The ovaries are the storehouses for a female's eggs, or ova (singular is ovum), all of which are present in her body at birth. There are probably between 300,000 and 400,000 of them in each baby girl. Commencing at puberty, which occurs in females between the ages of approximately twelve and fifteen, one egg ripens each month–alternating between the two ovaries. This process is known as ovulation. The ripened egg moves into the Fallopian tubes, which extend from the ovaries to the uterus, or womb. If sperm from a male happens to be in a female's vagina at the time a ripened egg is in the Fallopian tubes, it is attracted to the egg, penetrates and fertilizes it, and conception (another term for onset of pregnancy) has begun. As soon as a spermatozoon (singular of spermatozoa) has thus penetrated an egg, no other spermatozoon is able to do so.

If no sperm is present to fertilize the egg, the egg passes on down the vagina and is expelled from the body in a monthly flow of blood called menstruation. No one has ever actually seen the egg as it leaves the body. It is less than one-hundredth of an inch in diameter; about three million of them could be accommodated in a thimble.

Unlike the male urethra, there is no one passage in a female to carry both her urine and her sexual secretions. It is only near the mouth of the vagina that the outlet from the bladder reaches the same general outer opening from her body.

Just as some boys worry, especially during adolescence, about the size of their penises, girls may experience similar concern over their breasts. The size of a female's breasts is in no way related either to her own sexuality or to the probability of her being attractive; some males prefer large breasts, others small ones. Girls also sometimes worry because their breasts do not seem to be exactly the same size. This is of no greater consequence than that our arms, legs, hands, eyes, and ears also vary in their dimensions. None of us is precisely symmetrical.

*L*IFE BEGINS When an egg has been fertilized, it then normally moves into the womb, its home for the next nine months. There it slowly develops into a human infant, obtaining all its nourishment from the body of the mother. A human egg cell, at the moment it is fertilized, weighs a twenty-millionth of an ounce; after developing into an average adult, its weight has multiplied fifty billion times. Yet in that initial microscopic cell are contained all the physical, emotional, and spiritual potentialities of the adult!

DEVELOPMENT OF THE HUMAN EGG

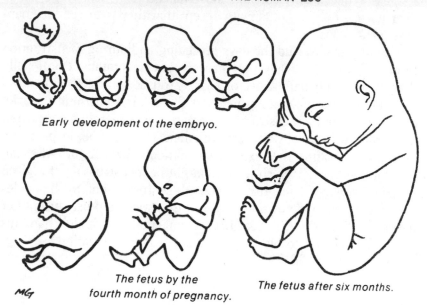

Early development of the embryo.

MG

*The fetus by the
fourth month of pregnancy.*

The fetus after six months.

Since a developing embryo derives all its nourishment from its mother's bloodstream, it is immensely important for a pregnant female to receive adequate, wholesome, balanced nutrition. We know now that the use of certain medications during pregnancy–even more, of tobacco, alcohol, or drugs like marijuana and cocaine–can severely damage a fetus and can result in the birth of a retarded, deformed, or handicapped infant.

The womb is the best possible host for the developing life it harbors. It is so anxious to perform its duties well that each month it prepares for a possible guest. As ovulation is about to take place, the walls of the womb thicken with extra blood supply, ready to feed the fertilized egg if it arrives. If no such guest makes an appearance that month, the nourishment provided in advance becomes unnecessary, sloughs off from the walls of the womb, and passes out through the vagina. This process, called menstruation, is often referred to as a female's *period*. Once she has reached puberty, a female menstruates each month unless she is pregnant. A small quantity of blood–usually half a cup or less–along with some of the mucus from the uterus wall, flows out of her body.

Menstruation can last anywhere from a couple of days to about a week. While it is occurring, most females can usually go about their normal routines of activity except that they wear sanitary napkins or tampons.

Some females find the days preceding and during menstruation to be difficult. Physically they may experience cramps: emotionally they may be unusually tense or easily aroused to anger or tears.

It was once universally believed there was something unlucky or unclean about a menstruating woman. It was therefore considered dangerous to have any contact with her. This may be, in part, the origin of separating the sexes in an Orthodox synagogue. After all, one could never tell which females might be menstruating at a given religious service. The great thirteenth-century rabbi Nachmanides prohibited a physician from even feeling his wife's pulse during her period.[1] And Rashi, the great Bible commentator, wouldn't hand his house key directly to his wife while she was menstruating.[2]

Today we recognize this to be sheer superstition. Ancient peoples are not to be condemned; they were operating with the limited knowledge of their time. There is no excuse, however, for a modern person to believe such nonsense. A menstruating female, provided she follows simple rules of hygiene to keep herself clean, is living through a perfectly natural phase of her life. She should be treated (and should treat herself) as normally as possible and is no more to be shunned or avoided than a person with a nosebleed.

Just as some boys begin to produce sperm earlier or later than the average, so there are girls whose menstruation commences sooner or later than in most cases. Usually a woman continues to menstruate monthly until she reaches the age of about forty-five to fifty-five. The stage at which menstruation gradually ceases is called menopause, or change of life. Thereafter, it is impossible for a woman to become pregnant. She can continue, however, to enjoy an active sex life.

*P*ERFECT UNION Few things on earth are as wondrous or mysterious as how a male and female create a new human being. Nature has provided for the perpetuation of all its species through reproduction.

Through sexual intercourse—also called coitus or copulation—humans become parents. The enlarged and stiffened penis is inserted into the vagina, which has also enlarged enough, through stimulation, to receive it. It is then moved back and forth, with increasing excitement, until the male comes to a climax known as an orgasm. When this happens, there is an ejaculation of semen in spurts. The contact between penis and vagina can induce an orgasm in the female, too, with much the same pleasurable physical sensation but with no ejaculation.

I have already mentioned that the clitoris is the most sexually sensitive part of the female anatomy. Stimulation of the clitoris brings about orgasm in the female. Some females are so sensitive that they are more effectively brought to climax when the clitoris is massaged indirectly, through neighboring tissue, than by direct contact.

Each sperm is so small that ten thousand or more, placed side by side, would cover less than an inch. Each also has a lashing tail, like a tadpole, that propels it to swim up into the vagina in the direction of the Fallopian tubes. If there is a ripened egg waiting there and just one sperm penetrates it, pregnancy has begun. If not, the sperm will gradually dry up or drain out of the vagina.

*W*HERE WE DIFFER Intercourse among human beings differs in a number of very important ways from the same phenomenon in other animals. Among these differences are the following:

1. With very few exceptions–dolphins and whales, for example–only among humans do the partners generally face and see each other during the act of intercourse.

2. Only among humans does intercourse serve purposes other than propagation of the race. It is doubtful whether females other than humans are even capable of experiencing an orgasm. Intercourse in the rest of the animal kingdom occurs only when the female is ready to be impregnated and only for the purpose of pregnancy. Intercourse in human life occurs when two people who love each other want thus to express their love. And, in addition to the fact that it sometimes results in pregnancy, in a good marriage it increases the very love it expresses.

3. Only among humans does intercourse have a spiritual as well as a physical aspect. Only with us does it lead to the formation of families and the creation of an attachment that can endure even beyond the time of life when intercourse between the partners may cease.

Some humans participate in sexual intercourse on a purely physical level. For others, however, sexual intercourse is an expression and reinforcement of lasting love–what might be called a bonding effect, strengthening and deepening the love that binds them to each other.

4. Thus far we have mentioned only how sex can be a wonderful and exalted experience among humans. There are other ways, however, in which it can also be degrading. We are the only species where the male can sometimes overpower his partner and force intercourse against his partner's will. Forced coitus is called rape. Thus, sex in human life can be either immeasurably glorious or unforgivably depraved. The choice is ours.

$\mathcal{S}$EX, YES; PREGNANCY, NO! Only human beings are capable, if they wish, of preventing intercourse from resulting in pregnancy. This is referred to as birth control, or contraception. It can be accomplished in several ways. The most common are:

1. for the male to wear a thin sheath called a condom (also a *rubber*) on his penis to prevent any sperm from entering the vagina. Properly used, condoms offer about 80 to 85 percent protection against pregnancy. If combined with a contraceptive jelly or foam, the effectiveness is increased to about 97 percent. An erect penis must be carefully inserted into the condom, with space enough left at the tip to accommodate semen. When the flaccid penis is withdrawn from the vagina after ejaculation, care must be taken not to allow the condom to come off and semen to enter the vagina. Condoms are also a fairly effective, though by no means perfect, protection against sexually transmitted diseases, including AIDS (especially if they are lubricated with Non-oxynol 9).

2. for the female to insert a diaphragm, a cervical cap that covers the opening between the vagina and the uterus, thus preventing sperm from fertilizing a ripened egg;

3. to use a medicinal jelly or contraceptive foam that, if injected into the vagina before intercourse, can kill sperm;

4. to have a physician insert a small copper or plastic ring in the womb (called an intrauterine device, or IUD) which, for some reason we do not yet fully understand, prevents conception.

All American manufacturers of IUDs ceased making them in 1985 because of several successful lawsuits claiming their users developed infections and/or permanent infertility. However, IUDs are still available in Canada and elsewhere, and it is still legal for American gynecologists to insert them.

5. for the female to take a pill, commonly containing estrogen, a female hormone, which prevents ovulation, thus making it impossible for an egg to be fertilized. The pill, however, is taken not just in anticipation of each act of intercourse but for twenty days of each month under the direction of a physician; otherwise it is not dependable. The contraceptive pill produces unpleasant side effects in some women, such as weight gain, and may be contraindicated with certain family histories of illness, such as cancer, but is considered by most experts to be both safe and effective if used properly. It provides 99 percent protection against pregnancy. However, because in

rare instances the pill may aggravate some health conditions, it should be taken only on the advice and under the supervision of a physician.

Experiments are currently under way on several additional birth control methods. As this is being written, however, none of them is ready for general use. One is a "morning after" injection or pill, which would be given to a female some hours after intercourse. Strictly speaking, this is more like abortion than birth control. It would not prevent conception but would force the fertilized egg to be discharged through her vagina instead of becoming embedded in her uterus and developing there.

One such medication, RU 486, developed in France, has been approved for general use in several European countries but not yet in the United States. As a matter of fact, research and experimentation in birth control methods lag far behind in this country, resulting in large part from opposition by both political and religious right-wing groups as well as American chemical companies fearful of malpractice suits.

Work is also in progress on a pill, which, taken only once a month, would protect a female against pregnancy for that time span and on a capsule that, inserted by needle, would prevent pregnancy until or unless it were removed.

Pending perfection of such a permanent method as the last, some men and women who are positive they will never want more children resort to a surgical procedure called sterilization. If a female's Fallopian tubes are cut or tied, she can continue to have intercourse but will never become pregnant. The same objective is achieved in a male by an operation known as a vasectomy, in which the vasa deferentia are cut, preventing any passage of semen into his urethra. The danger of sterilization is that, should the individuals change their mind about having children, such surgery is difficult, if not impossible, to reverse.

*N*OT RECOMMENDED In addition to the birth control methods described above–all reasonably effective if properly used, the pill being most dependable–other methods are extremely unreliable. Boys, for example, have been known to use crude, home-made condoms, fashioned from rubber balloons or plastic wrap. Such substitutes provide virtually no protection. Even a professionally manufactured condom can fail if it contains so much as a microscopic hole or if it slips off the penis during intercourse.

A diaphragm, to provide protection, must be fitted for size by a physician, who also gives instruction on how to insert it and how long after intercourse to keep it in. It is also best to combine a diaphragm with a contraceptive jelly or foam.

Some women rely on douching after intercourse–washing out the vagina with a device similar to an enema bag in order to remove any sperm that may have been deposited there. Because a douche has a limited range, and especially because sperm are energetic enough to reach beyond that range toward the uterus before a douche can be used, this is among the least reliable methods of birth control.

One of the oldest known methods of birth control consists of inserting into the vagina a sponge to absorb semen, thus preventing sperm from entering the Fallopian tubes. This method is clearly described and recommended in the Talmud. Its modern adaptation, combined with a spermicide, is of unknown effectiveness–that is, not very reliable.

Another of the least reliable methods is the so-called rhythm method. This method is based on there being certain days in the menstrual cycle when no ripened egg is present, hence no possibility of becoming pregnant. While this is true, there is enough variation in ovulation and menstruation in any one female to make the calculation of this safe period so complicated that it cannot be used with any great assurance.

An extremely unreliable method that some couples foolishly use is called coitus interruptus, or withdrawal. This means commencing coitus but not completing it; as soon as the male feels his orgasm beginning, he quickly withdraws his penis from the vagina to prevent sperm from entering the female's body. In addition to being an unhealthfully frustrating practice for both sexes, coitus interruptus is undependable as a method of birth control because sometimes semen begins to flow from the penis even before the actual orgasm. The attraction of sperm for a ripened egg, moreover, is so great that even when deposited outside a female's body, near the lips of her vagina, they can swim toward the Fallopian tubes and cause conception. There have been females who became pregnant in this manner without actually experiencing intercourse.

*I*N THE TALMUD The Talmud prescribes birth control in some circumstances. The following advice appears no less than six times in rabbinic literature, five times in the Talmud, once in *Tosefta*:

> There are three women who, when experiencing sex relations with their husbands, may (or must) take the precaution of using an absorbent to prevent conception: a minor, a pregnant woman, and a woman who is still nursing her baby.[3]

What were our ancient teachers really attempting to tell us in this passage? Three things: that the prevention of pregnancy in a minor was permissible to safeguard the health of the prospective mother and child; that it was legitimate in the case of a woman already pregnant, again for the sake both of mother and child; that it was acceptable when a mother was still nursing, for the welfare of a child already born. The explanations of Rashi and other commentators on this passage allow no room for doubt. The only area of potential disagreement is whether, under any of the foregoing circumstances, a woman *may* or *must* use contraception. It is also clear from the opinions of medieval and premodern rabbis that birth control was deemed permissible when a woman had already given birth to children who were mentally retarded or suffered from an incurable congenital disease.

There are Jews—even some rabbis—who oppose contraception. Their opposition may be owing to a misunderstanding of the tradition or to uneasiness over sex despite the tradition or to a legitimate fear that, if we Jews approach zero-population growth, especially after six million of us were exterminated during the Holocaust, we may risk our disappearance as an identifiable people. The modern Jew confronts a most painful predicament between a knowledge that the human population of the earth must be curbed if disaster is to be averted, and an insistence that it is important—for us and for all humankind—that we Jews survive.

*M*URDERER! MURDERER? You have doubtless seen television shots of hordes marching in angry protest in front of abortion clinics. Those who object to abortion and want the law to prohibit it claim they support the "right to life," a slogan that is misleading. These people often picket abortion clinics, even violently blocking the entrance to prevent women from keeping their appointments. In a few cases the protesters have even been arrested and convicted of deliberately setting fires and destroying files at such institutions.

Those who call themselves "pro-choice" insist that a pregnant woman should have the right to choose whether to go through with the birth or abort her fetus.

Abortion and birth control are quite different; although both prevent the development and birth of a child, contraception accomplishes this by preventing the fertilization of an egg, abortion by removing a fetus from the womb after it has begun to develop. This is usually done by a relatively simple surgical procedure through the vagina, during which the walls of the uterus are scraped, thus removing the fetus. Abortion can also be accomplished by use of suction or injection of a saline solution. The best and safest time is before the tenth week of pregnancy; after that, abortion becomes increasingly risky. Beyond a certain point the operation can no longer be done through the vagina but requires an abdominal incision.

Until only a few years ago abortion was declared illegal by every state in this nation. As a result, some females, driven to desperation by the discovery that they were pregnant, either tried to induce abortion themselves or sought illegal abortions. In the hope of accomplishing the former, they would use something like a bleach or a coat hanger or violent exercise. All such methods, in addition to being highly ineffective, are horribly dangerous. The procedures followed by illegal abortionists aren't much better, often resulting in severe infections, profuse bleeding, sterility, or even death. Performed in a hospital by a competent physician at the proper stage of pregnancy, abortion is a safe procedure with almost no risk.

In 1973 the Supreme Court of the United States decreed that during the first third of her pregnancy, no law could deny a woman the right to have a medically supervised abortion if she and her physician agreed on its advisability. In 1989 that same court–by then transformed into a much more conservative body by several Reagan appointments–ruled that states might, if they wished, severely restrict a woman's right to abortions. The nation is still polarized between the supporters of pro-choice and of so-called pro-life.

The latter claim that a human life begins at the very instant of conception, rendering abortion "the murder of an unborn child."

The Catholic Church and some other religious denominations

are vigorously opposed to abortion, perhaps even more than to birth control. The rejection of abortion by some people is highly emotional. Shortly after stating on television my view that under certain circumstances abortion should be allowed, I received a hysterical letter from a man who, among other things, wrote: "It is most disturbing that child murder has the support of a person whose authority should be lent to the cause of decency. Your espousal of abortion puts you in company with those who ran the concentration camps of Nazi Germany. . . .The fact that you are a rabbi evinces the decay of Judaism as a moral force."

How do you react to these words? Do you agree that abortion is to be equated with child murder? With the exterminations at German concentration camps? Under what circumstances would you justify abortion? Is it the best alternative?

Judaism does not agree with the Catholic position on abortion. Our rabbis never considered the fetus to be a נֶפֶשׁ *nefesh*, a human being with a soul. Until it had been actually born, legally and morally the fetus was considered part of the potential mother's body, like one of her limbs. According to some interpretations of talmudic law, if a רוֹדֵף *rodef*, a pursuer, threatens my life and the only way I can possibly save myself is to kill him first, I am justified in doing so. In any situation where a continuation of pregnancy would jeopardize the life of a mother, the same principle was applied; the fetus is viewed as a רוֹדֵף; its life is secondary to that of the mother and is to be sacrificed, if necessary, in order to save hers.

Suppose there is no immediate physical threat to the mother's life? Here the ancient rabbis are not of a single mind; some are liberal, others strict in judging the matter. Even the strictest, however, agree that, if continued pregnancy would cause extreme mental anguish to the mother, so serious as to carry a threat of either suicide or hysteria on her part, abortion is allowed. In 1913 an Orthodox responsum (rabbinic reply to a request for a legal judgment) dealt with the specific case of a pregnant woman whose mental health was at stake. It decreed:

> Mental health risk has been definitely equated to physical health risk. This woman who is in danger of losing her mental health unless the pregnancy is interrupted would accordingly qualify.

Similarly, if a pregnant woman is anguished almost to the point of mental breakdown or suicide, over the possibility that delivering another child might harm one already born or that the fetus she carries may prove to be a defective child, some Orthodox rabbinic authorities would uphold her right to abort.

There are some Orthodox rabbis, though, whose views on abortion are scarcely distinguishable from the Catholic position. They are inclined to oppose it under all but the most extreme circumstances. It seems to me that they thus depart radically from the liberalism of genuinely traditional Judaism. In a curiously paradoxical way it is sometimes possible for a non-Orthodox Jew to reflect the spirit of Jewish tradition more accurately on a specific matter than do some Orthodox Jews. That spirit clearly allows abortion where the physical or mental health of a mother would otherwise be threatened.

This should not be misinterpreted to mean that Judaism looks lightly upon abortion or would approve of abortion merely for reasons of convenience. Our tradition approves birth control; this, not abortion, is the recognized way for a couple to enjoy intercourse without producing a child. Yet, under special circumstances such as those described above, abortion is considered acceptable.

Some women–probably not as many now as in the past–suffer serious emotional stress after having an abortion. At the very least, a woman who is contemplating such a step should have the benefit of skilled and sensitive professional counseling both before and after her abortion.

Studies have shown that about 43 percent of pregnant teenagers resort to abortion. Although the pregnancy rate for blacks is about twice that of whites, the percentage of both groups who choose abortion is the same. As of 1989, twenty-six states required that parents give their consent or at least be informed before a teenage pregnancy could be terminated. Other states permit this only if a judge approves. It has been estimated that about 65 percent of pregnant teenage girls do confide in one or both parents.[4]

Do you think the law should require parental or judicial consent for teenage abortion? If the teenager is married, should the consent of her husband be required? How about the consent or knowledge of the one who impregnated her if she is unmarried? What might determine whether or not a teenager would tell her parents?

NOTES

SEX: FICTION AND FACT

1. *Bet Yosef, Tur Y.D.* 195.
2. *Tosafot, Shabbat* 13b.
3. *Yevamot* 12b, 108b; *Ketubot* 39a; *Niddah* 45a; *Nedarim* 35b; *Tosefta Niddah* II.
4. *The New York Times,* July 16, 1989.

THE MORNING AFTER

Three years ago Louise experienced the only sexual indiscretion of her life. She had been dating Charlie for nearly a year when one romantic night, before either of them realized what was happening, their petting resulted in intercourse. It was an extremely distasteful episode for her, one she resolved never to repeat. And she had kept her resolution with both of the young men she had dated since then, including Allan, to whom she is now engaged. She told him nothing of the earlier event nor that she had become pregnant but, with the help of a nurse she knew, had an abortion early in her pregnancy.

As the date of her wedding to Allan approached, she found herself increasingly troubled. Should she tell him or not? If she did, she might lose him. If she did not, Louise might always regret that she had deceived her husband. Though she had been a calm kind of person most of her life, lately she hasn't been able to sleep well because of this worry.

What should Louise do? Why? What will be the probable consequences of keeping this episode to herself? Of telling it to Allan? Is there a perfect solution?

Louise is by no means the only person to have discovered that, while sex can be truly wonderful, it can also result in great distress and pain. Nor is she the only one to have learned that decisions we make today are likely to affect our lives tomorrow. The purpose of this chapter is not to frighten you about sex but to help you appreciate the priceless gift you have been given and to maximize the joys of sex while minimizing its potential pain.

Sometimes it seems our entire culture has conspired to reduce sex to a commodity exchanged for easy favors. Our most popular movies and television programs show impassioned couples hopping into and out of bed, with never a thought of love or responsibility or commitment. One family planning group has estimated that in 1986 alone television programs in the United States portrayed no fewer than twenty-thousand instances of "suggested sexual intercourse" without a single mention of birth control or disease prevention. It's impossible to check out of a supermarket–or even to read the average daily newspaper–without being assaulted by lurid stories of incest, adultery, and rape. The advertising industry on this continent exploits photographs of scantily-clad women to sell everything from automobiles to toothpaste. For every time you have been exposed in public film or print to the idea that sex is sacred, there have been a thousand or more suggestions that sex is sordid and cheap. This is both a source and a result of the pains that so often accompany our sexual behavior.

$\mathcal{B}$RUTAL ASSAULT Only we humans are capable of committing rape. If a male dog attempts to copulate with an unwilling female, she will resist him ferociously, even biting off his testicles if that is her only means of protection.

We usually associate rape with an image of females attacked in their apartments by robbers or while jogging alone in a park. In actuality, most rapes are committed by males who are known to their victims. Some rapes occur when a couple, petting on an ordinary date, go further than they had intended, and the male forces intercourse on his unwilling date. Forcing sex on an unwilling person is never excusable; its inevitable consequence is pain, both physical and emotional, both immediate and lasting.

One authority reports: "In one survey of women on thirty-two college campuses, 15 percent had experienced at least one rape, and 89 percent of the time it was by men the women knew. Half the rapes occurred during a date."

Marital rape is also possible. Husbands have been known to impose intercourse on unwilling wives. In recent years there have even been several lawsuits based on such accusations. Such incidents are a gross violation not a fulfillment of the couple's marriage vows.

Most students of sexual behavior are convinced that rape evidences sheer violence, aggression, and contempt of women.

*U*NWELCOME CONSEQUENCES Another source of pain resulting from sexual behavior is unwanted pregnancy. It's hard to believe how many teenagers, even those who know about contraception, fail to use any birth control method when having intercourse. It has been estimated that half of all sexually active teenagers in this country don't use contraception at first intercourse; 25 percent never use it; only about one-third do so regularly. This is despite the fact that 20 percent of all premarital pregnancies happen in the first month of intercourse and 50 percent in the first six months.[1]

One of the most authentic and reliable surveys of teenage sexual behavior in the United States was done in the mid-1980s by *Rolling Stone* magazine. Its results were published by Drs. Robert Coles and Geoffrey Stokes, who write: "Behind the words on these pages stand 1,067 questionnaires with 358 variables, 50,000 pages of transcribed interviews, several miles of computer printouts, and a formidable array of academic and clinical experience."[2] Among the seventeen-year-old females included in this survey 31 percent had been pregnant, among the eighteen-year-olds, 22 percent. Not incidentally 86 percent of these pregnancies had terminated in abortions.

It has been reliably estimated that more than a million teenage pregnancies occur in the United States annually, by far the highest rate in any industrialized nation. Our rate here in 1980 was 96 per thousand, compared to 45 in England and Wales, 35 in Sweden, 14 in the Netherlands. This difference can undoubtedly be attributed at least in part to our society's attitudes on sex and to the other countries' offering their young people far more extensive public courses in sex education. Our rate of teenage abortions in this country matches or exceeds the combined rates of abortions and births in five other of the world's most advanced nations.[3]

Statistics can be both instructive and convincing. They cannot reveal, though, nor must they ever be allowed to conceal, the immeasurable amount of heartache and anguish unwanted pregnancy and abortion often bring to the young women involved, to their parents, and to the men who impregnated them.

Who are the young girls in this country most likely to become pregnant? A 1986 study by the Children's Defense Fund in Washington provides the answer:
• Girls with poor basic skills are five times more likely to become mothers before age sixteen than those with average skills.
• Those with poor or average basic skills have three or four times the probability of having more than one child while still in their teens than those with average skills.

By way of further explanation: "Many disadvantaged youths sense they have nothing to lose by becoming parents. They feel no door will be closed by teen pregnancy because they believe from the outset that no doors are open to them. . . . [They] are the youngsters whose academic shortcomings and concomitant low self-esteem make them, in their own eyes, failures even in comparison with their socio-economic peers."[4]

Two of every three teenagers who become pregnant fail to finish high school; teenage married parents with children are far more likely to separate or divorce than those who postpone parenthood; the income of teen mothers averages half that of those who first become mothers in their twenties.

*S*ICK, SICK, SICK! Even worse than the pain caused by unwanted pregnancy is that of sexually transmitted diseases (STDs). Two of the most commonly known are syphilis and gonorrhea. One-fourth of the million cases of gonorrhea occurring in the United States each year are found among teenagers.[5] These diseases are transmitted from one person to another almost exclusively through intercourse. They can result in blindness, deformed children, paralysis, sterility, and mental deterioration. In order to secure a marriage license it is now necessary in some states first to have one's blood tested to make sure neither party suffers from syphilis. But there is no way in the world of insuring that a partner in premarital coitus is free from infection.

Here again, there are some who minimize the danger, claiming we now have drugs that can control and even cure these diseases. Though we do have such medication, successful cures depend on early diagnosis and treatment. In many cases the disease is not recognized until early treatment is impossible. New strains of gonorrhea are resistant to the antibiotics that were expected until recently to have solved the problem. The herpes simplex virus, another STD, doesn't respond to antibiotics at all; there is currently no cure for it. Resulting largely from the increased abuse of illegal drugs, even syphilis, which health officials thought they were capable of wiping out, has reappeared as a major threat. The number of cases reported in the United States, 6,392 in 1947, had risen by 1988 to 40,117.

Despite our vaunted medical progress, STDs still pose a frightening prospect. The incidence of chancroid, a genital ulcer disease affecting predominantly males, increased seven-and-a-half times between 1982 and 1986. Between 1983 and 1988 the number of children born in this country with syphilis increased 4.7 times.

Teenagers seem to be especially susceptible to STDs. It has been estimated that one out of four Americans between the ages of fifteen and fifty-five will at some point contract an STD, 85 percent of them in the age span of fifteen to thirty. Many teenagers will fall prey to chlamydia, the fastest-growing sexual disease in the United States today. Though its symptoms may be minor or even unrecognizable, in females it can cause pelvic inflammatory disease and infertility; in males it often leads to infertility also; worst of all, it can afflict newborn babies, leading to blindness or fatal pneumonia. Similarly disastrous maladies can be caused in newborns by a disease known as venereal warts.[6]

NO CURE, LITTLE CHANCE How can I best describe the danger of AIDS (Acquired Immune Deficiency Syndrome)? Among the many wondrous physiological features of the human body is its automatic line of defense, the immune system. Whenever infection invades the body the white corpuscles in the bloodstream immediately mobilize to defend against the invading bacteria.

Similarly the body has the amazing automatic capacity to create antibodies against the germs of nearly any disease that invades it. Some of our most effective vaccinations and inoculations consist of the deliberate injection of specific germs in a quantity not sufficient actually to infect us with the disease but enough to stimulate the development of natural antibodies to protect us against that disease, often long into the future if not permanently.

No one dies directly from AIDS. No one survives a fully developed case of AIDS, either. This is because the attacking virus, Human Immunodeficiency Virus (HIV), destroys the body's capacity to create antibodies, thus rendering the victim powerless against a number of lethal diseases, among them pneumonia and certain kinds of cancer.

The first cases of AIDS in the United States were diagnosed in 1981. By the middle of 1987 at least thirty-three-thousand cases had been identified and over half of the afflicted had already died. According to the most reliable current estimates, there will be at least two-hundred-seventy-thousand cases in this country by 1991. Of the million-and-a-half to three million individuals in the U.S. who were probably carrying the AIDS virus in 1989, 20 to 30 percent will develop AIDS, and nearly all of these will die. Despite frantic medical research there is as yet no known cure.

There are, to be sure, blood tests that can disclose whether a given individual does or does not carry the AIDS virus. These tests, however, are not as readily definitive as had at first been hoped, for the virus can incubate in a person probably for as long as ten years before any symptoms appear. In some cases, moreover, the tests may not reveal the virus's presence until six months or more after infection has commenced. Thus a person who is carrying the virus may test as if uninfected. Still, it is extremely important for any sexually active person to be periodically tested.

What are the symptoms of AIDS? Among them are: chronic fatigue, fever, chills, night sweats, inexplicable weight loss of more than ten pounds, and pink or purple bumps beneath the skin that

persist for more than two weeks. This doesn't mean that a person who manifests any of these symptoms necessarily has AIDS: these are simply the warning signs of possible trouble.

How does one become infected by the AIDS virus? *Not* by shaking hands, social kissing, coughing or sneezing, sharing cups, dishes, bed linens, towels, toilets, telephones. Not by any of these, nor by insect bites.

The primary source of infection is through sexual intercourse with one already infected, through receiving contaminated blood by transfusion, from an infected mother to her unborn child, by sharing narcotic needles with an infected individual. Some drug dealers have even been known to wipe off used needles, then repackage and sell them as new, though they remain contaminated.

I have already mentioned the special vulnerability of young people to sexually transmitted diseases in general. Recent research shows this to include AIDS. Between 1987 and 1989 the number of AIDS cases reported in teenagers increased by 40 percent. It is likely that many additional cases were not reported. The Center for Disease Control in Atlanta reported in late 1989 that 20 percent of all males diagnosed with AIDS and 25 percent of females were still in their twenties. This means that most of them actually contracted the disease in their teens; the average time span between infection with HIV and development of AIDS is ten years.[7]

There is only one certain way of protecting yourself against AIDS: to desist from all the risks described above. To abstain from sexual intercourse or, failing that, to indulge only with a person who has never had intercourse with anyone else, or never to have intercourse without using a condom (especially one lubricated with Nonoxynol 9, which kills the AIDS virus). There is no way to be absolutely certain a potential sexual partner is virus-free because (a) you have only his or her word there has been no previous exposure and (b) even AIDS testing is by no means 100 percent reliable. Remember also that using a condom reduces the risk but definitely does not erase it. An additional minor but important caution: Refrain from all tattooing and, if you have your ears pierced, be sure it is done only with sterile equipment.

Although AIDS cases do appear among heterosexuals, the largest population afflicted has been male homosexuals. This has greatly aggravated the fear of and animosity toward homosexuals that existed even before we knew of AIDS.

The decision about whether sex in your life will be a source of great blessing or of blighting curse–or a mediocre experience somewhere between these extremes–is entirely yours. Others can attempt to influence that choice, but no one else can make it for you.

Anger, too, is a natural human impulse that can be used constructively or destructively. Anger directed habitually toward other individuals or yourself can destroy you. Anger aimed at injustice, at prejudice and discrimination, at those in power trampling on the powerless–that kind of anger can make you into a better, more creative, more productive person.

So it is with sex. And remember: the decisions you make today, tomorrow, next month, and next year will have a great effect on the quality of your sex life and love after you marry.

*S*EX FOR ONE If you're male, the overwhelming probability is that you have masturbated; close to 100 percent of all males have. The percentage of females who have masturbated is but slightly less. Male or female, you undoubtedly know that masturbation–also commonly referred to as *jerking off, whacking off,* or *getting off*–consists of manipulating the penis or clitoris, by hand or with some other object, usually to the point of orgasm.

Probably more guilt has been incurred about masturbation than any other area. Until recently masturbation had been proscribed by both medical and religious leadership. Among the alleged consequences, against which generations of boys in particular have been sternly warned, are: blotched skin, tuberculosis, dyspepsia, heart disease, epilepsy, blindness, paralysis, insanity, and sexual impotence. Quite a list! That not even this false catalog of catastrophes succeeded in eliminating the practice of masturbation attests to the strength of the sex drive.

This again is one of the matters on which liberal Jews must respect our tradition without necessarily following it. Most of the ethical insights of Judaism are at least as valid today as when they were first conceived by our ancestors. In some areas, however, because we have knowledge that was unavailable to them, we must revise or even discard their judgments. The same is true with reference to the treatment of certain diseases. Were we to limit ourselves now to the medical knowledge and procedures of those who wrote the Torah and Talmud, we would obviously be handicapping ourselves in our endeavor to maintain and improve health.

So it is with masturbation. Limited to the knowledge of those who so sternly warned against it in the past, we would doubtless feel exactly as they did. But we are not so limited. Medical and psychiatric experts are unanimously agreed that masturbation is *not* harmful; it does *not* cause any of the disasters once attributed to it. The only harm resulting from masturbation is the profound but unwarranted sense of guilt it has induced in the past.

Once this unjustifiable guilt is removed, far from being harmful, masturbation may even be advisable. Through it, young people may learn to achieve orgasm and find a way to relieve their sexual tensions without inviting into their lives some of the dangers and risks involved in premarital intercourse. Females, who sometimes experience difficulty in reaching an orgasm, can discover through masturbation just what pressures and motions on the clitoris are best calculated to bring them to a sexual climax. Males, who find it much easier and more natural to reach orgasm, can learn through masturbation how to delay it, a technique that may be invaluable later when it becomes necessary to slow down their own progress in coitus so that their partners may match their degree of arousal.

Usually a person who is masturbating fantasizes or daydreams about being involved in a sexual incident. He or she may view an erotic picture, read a sexy passage in a book, or just rely on imagination. There is no more reason to feel guilty about such fantasies than about masturbation itself. Judaism does not equate thought with act, fantasy with deed. So long as sexual fantasies do not permanently and entirely replace reality, they can serve a useful purpose in our sexual development.

Sometimes masturbation is accompanied by viewing pornographic pictures, photographs of nudes or seminudes or even of couples engaged in sexual contact. These may appear together with verbal descriptions of sexual encounters. Many magazines contain such material; they are available on most newsstands.

Is it wrong to use pornography in this way? Not really–though a word of caution is in order. This kind of literature and photography nearly always cheapens sex and degrades females, if not males as well. Most pornography deals with sex only on the crudest, purely physical level. It makes the human body, a wonderfully beautiful creation, into an object of display, often exaggerating its physical dimensions and describing intercourse as a purely animalistic kind of experience. It portrays sex as something one person does *to* another for his or her own gratification, not as an experience shared by two people to express and enhance their love and intimacy. There is little room for tenderness or mutual commitment or love in pornography. Unless we include a great deal of tenderness and mutual commitment and love in our sexual lives we fail to become fully human.

*O*N THE FRINGES I have tried in this chapter to describe various expressions of sexuality. There are still a few additional manifestations of sexuality, which, though relatively rare, are important to know.

Exhibitionism means the desire or need of an individual to display his or her genitals in public. Exhibitionists are usually inadequate, insecure people who hope to shock others. The most effective way of dealing with them is to ignore them. Seldom do they become aggressive or act out their sexual desires.

Voyeurism is the technical term referring to the actions of those we more commonly call "peeping toms," men or women (more often the former) who derive sexual pleasure from watching others in the nude or in the act of intercourse.

Transvestism refers to the practice of wearing the clothing of the opposite sex. Though we are not yet sure what causes this kind of behavior, we do know it is not necessarily an indication of homosexuality.

Transsexualism, also called *sex-role inversion*, designates the condition of individuals who prefer to be members of the opposite sex. From time to time such individuals actually resort to plastic surgery in order to accomplish their desires.

Bestiality is the practice of having intercourse with animals. For obvious reasons, this is likely to be found more often among farm than city denizen.

*W*HAT'S NORMAL Thoughtless people might immediately assume that whatever they themselves do sexually is normal, everything else abnormal. What would be more reasonable to say is that any form of sexual behavior between consenting adults–forced upon no one, repugnant to no one–is acceptable for those people.

*L*ESBIANS AND GAYS Homosexuality may involve either two men or two women who achieve their sexual satisfaction together. They may experience orgasm either through mutual masturbation or, in the instance of males, through insertion of the penis of one into the anus of the other or through oral-genital contact. Female homosexuals are called lesbians. The word *gay*, sometimes used for both male and female homosexuals, usually refers to males. Common, vulgar terms for female homosexuals are *butch* or *dyke*; males are sometimes called *fairies, faggots, fags*, or *queers*. (Because all these labels are generally used in a prejudiced or derisive way, we should avoid using them.) This is another area where the wildest and weirdest kind of emotional, even hysterical, reactions are often heard. Surely the better part of both wisdom and humaneness is to approach the subject as rationally as we can.

Some individuals are bisexual, able to enjoy sexual relations with members of either sex. There are also some who, though generally heterosexual, may be driven to homosexual behavior under such restrictive circumstances as being in the army or in prison, where contact is possible only with members of their own sex.

Though there is still so much about this phenomenon that we do not know, it occurs quite commonly in the animal world in cows, monkeys, and chimpanzees, among others. It is purported that often homosexuality in humans is accompanied by a high degree of artistic sensitivity. Among the famous men who are said to have been homosexuals are Leonardo da Vinci, Michelangelo, Tchaikovsky, and Walt Whitman. It is a mistake to assume homosexuals are always identifiable by their mannerisms. Very masculine-looking male professional athletes as well as quite feminine females have been known to be homosexual.

There are as many different kinds of homosexuals as heterosexuals; both can be either healthy or neurotic. Homosexual couples often live together in a stable, loving relationship.

Rabbi Yoel H. Kahn, spiritual leader of a San Francisco congregation, most of whose members are lesbian and gay, expressed the following sentiments in a June 1989 address to the Central Conference of American Rabbis:

> When I arrived in San Francisco four years ago, deep down I believed that gay and lesbian relationships and families were, somehow, not as real, not as stable, not as committed, as heterosexual marriages. I could tell many stories of what I have learned. There are the two women who have lived together for many years without familial or communal support, who have endured long distances and job transfers because employers thought them both single, and admitting their homosexuality would have endangered their livelihoods, women who have cared for each other without benefit of insurance coverage or health benefits or any legal protection. They came to me one Friday night and simply asked: "Rabbi, this is our twenty-fifth anniversary; will you say a blessing?"
>
> Mine is a synagogue living with AIDS. I have been humbled by the unquestioning devotion of one of our members who, for more than two years, went to work each morning, calling intermittently throughout the day to check in on his partner, and spent each night comforting, talking, preparing meals, and waking in the middle of the night to carry his lover to the bathroom. . . . The loving caregiver stayed at his partner's side throughout the period of his illness and until his death.

The amount of prejudice and discrimination our society has aimed at known homosexuals is astounding. They have been hounded and harassed, fired from their jobs or denied employment, maimed by violent attack, expelled from hospitals and schools, and driven from their communities and homes. In some ways their plight resembles that of fourteenth-century Jews who were irrationally, insanely accused of causing half of Europe's population to die in the Black Death plague. Surely our Jewish ethic demands that we protect the lives and rights of homosexuals as fully as we do those of heterosexuals.

The Union of American Hebrew Congregations has adopted vigorous resolutions urging such action. In 1974 the Union of American Hebrew Congregations was faced with a difficult dilemma when a congregation consisting predominantly though not exclusively of homosexuals applied for admission. After prolonged debate on a very high level, the UAHC Board of Trustees accepted the application. Since then several similar congregations have been admitted to the Union.

The most recent resolution, passed near the end of 1989, states that every Reform congregation "must be a place where loneliness, suffering, and exile end, where gay and lesbian Jews can know that they are accepted on terms of visibility, not invisibility; that we place no limits on their communal or spiritual aspirations."

Recognizing that homosexual relationships at their best can be as loving and lasting as Rabbi Kahn describes them, Sweden and Denmark have enacted legislation giving homosexual couples many of the advantages and rights that have always been enjoyed by heterosexual married couples. These include tax benefits, insurance and alimony privileges, and provisions for property inheritance. Nothing so sweeping as this has taken place yet in the United States, though in 1989 New York State's highest court ruled that under the rent-control law the survivor after the death of one member in a gay or lesbian relationship that has lasted at least a decade must be given the same protection afforded when one partner in a heterosexual marriage has died.

In 1990, after four years of intensive study, the Central Conference of American Rabbis adopted a resolution urging that acknowledged homosexuals who are properly qualified be afforded the same opportunities as heterosexuals to serve in the rabbinate. While endorsing the traditional Jewish value of heterosexual relationships leading to procreation, the resolution also recommended that congregations open their pulpits to homosexuals.

What do you think of the New York State court ruling? About

*accepting acknowledged homosexuals as rabbis? How would you feel
if your rabbi were lesbian or gay? Do you think this would encourage
homosexuality among the young people in your congregation?*

There is no truth whatever to the frequently expressed fear that
gay men are particularly inclined to assault or entice innocent young
boys sexually. Such attacks do, indeed, occasionally occur, but by
far more heterosexuals than homosexuals commit these crimes.

Any young person who has persistently strong feelings of
attraction to someone of the same sex would be well advised to con-
sult someone who is both knowledgeable and trustworthy. Here, as
in all areas of sexual development, our greatest enemy is
ignorance.

*S*LAVES TO THE PAST For many reasons, not the
least of which are the obvious implications for the future of
the family, Judaism has traditionally opposed and rejected homosexuality. The subject is mentioned in the story of Sodom, a city whose
men demanded of Lot that he surrender his male guests to become
victims of gang rape.[8] What is only hinted or suggested earlier
becomes directly prohibited by law in the Book of Leviticus: "If a
man lies with a male as one lies with a woman, the two of them have
done an abhorrent thing; they shall be put to death–their bloodguilt
is upon them."[9]

Here again the attitude of liberal Judaism differs considerably
from that of ancient Jewish tradition. My own strong feeling is that,
so long as a homosexual relationship is between consenting adults,
so long as no one is being forced or coerced, it is not society's business to interfere.

This squares with a widespread change in the attitude of American society as a whole. Owing in no small measure to the Gay Liberation movement, homosexuals have been encouraged to discard their
former feelings of secrecy and shame, to declare themselves for what
they are, and to insist on obtaining their rights. However we may
differ in our attitudes on the subject, there is little room for disagreement among enlightened individuals that homosexuals are at the
very least entitled to equality in every respect.

Rabbi Janet Marder, who formerly served a largely homosexual
congregation, has spoken movingly on the issue of reinterpreting
Jewish tradition regarding homosexuality:

... And so I had to decide: how much did it matter to me that the voice of my tradition, without exception, ran counter to the evidence of my experience and the deepest promptings of my conscience?

For me the choice was clear. I could not be guided by laws that seem profoundly unjust and immoral. I believe, and I teach my congregants, that Jewish law condemns their way of life. But I teach also that I cannot accept that law as authoritative. . . . In my view, the Jewish condemnation of homosexuality is the work of human beings—limited, imperfect, fearful of what is different. . . . In short, I think our ancestors were wrong about a number of things, and homosexuality is one of them.[10]

How do you feel about Rabbi Marder's view? Would any Orthodox or Conservative rabbi agree with her? Do all Reform rabbis agree with her? How can she or any other Reoform rabbi judge which rabbinic laws to accept and which to reject? If every rabbi is entitled to make such decisions, doesn't that risk eventual disappearance of the entire rabbinic tradition?

If you wish to know more about homosexuality, I recommend a book written especially for your age group, Morton Hunt's *Gay–What You Should Know about Homosexuality* (New York: Farrar, Straus & Giroux, 1977). Further information on this topic may also be obtained from: National Gay Task Force, 80 Fifth Ave., New York, NY 10011 or Parents and Friends of Lesbians and Gays, P.O. Box 24565, Los Angeles, CA 90024.

*W*HAT DO YOU THINK? Elaine, thirty-three years old and married eleven years, doesn't have a very good sex life with her husband, who is her senior by fourteen years. His desire for sex doesn't come close to matching hers. When they do have intercourse, sometimes she fails to achieve an orgasm; at other times, she does reach a climax but feels the need for more. By this time, however, her husband, having had his orgasm, is likely to be sound asleep. Knowing that men reach the highest point of their sexual potential in their late teens, Elaine has been making overtures to Don, a nineteen-year-old college student living across the street. So far this has amounted only to flirtation, but she is hoping to establish a sexual relationship with Don, expecting that they may be sexually more compatible than she and her husband are.

Evaluate Elaine's feelings and hopes. What consequences can you foresee if she continues on her plan? Can you suggest better alternatives? What about Don? What does he have to gain or lose in this situation?

Sally is one of the most popular girls in her high school. Extremely attractive, she has more requests for dates than she can possibly accept. One reason for this, she believes, is that she tries to let every boy who dates her have a good time. They all seem eager to pet, and she allows them to do so. Even when she may not enjoy the experience herself, she derives much satisfaction from knowing that, as a woman, she can attract and please men.

Other girls in her school, knowing something of her reputation, are quick to criticize her immorality and to accuse her of being promiscuous. This, however, is not true. Sally is a virgin and intends to remain one. She prides herself on knowing how far to go and when to stop. The moment she senses her date is on the verge of going too far, immediately she puts a stop to their petting. She feels she is always in control. So long as this is so, Sally considers herself a moral person.

What do you think? Is she moral? Are the girls who criticize her moral? Is it necessary for a girl to permit or encourage petting in order to be popular? For a boy to initiate sexual activity on dates in order to prove himself a man? Does a girl feel unwanted or rejected if her date doesn't "make a pass at her"?

NOTES
THE MORNING AFTER

1. *The New York Times*, August 29, 1989.
2. R. Coles and G. Stokes, *Sex and the American Teenager* (New York: Harper & Row, 1985), p. vii.
3. *Education Week*, March 20, 1985.
4. C. Cassell, *Straight from the Heart* (New York: Simon & Schuster, 1987), p. 21.
5. *Ibid.*, p. 191.
6. *Ibid.*, p. 197.
7. *The New York Times*, October 8, 1989.
8. Genesis 19:5.
9. Leviticus 18:22 and 20:13.
10. *The Reconstructionist*, October/November 1985.

GENDER DIFFERENCES

Though Joan has been married four years, she has never experienced an orgasm. At first she was sexually aroused to a high pitch when she and her husband went to bed together. Gradually that changed. Because Mark always *came* very quickly, she failed to climax, which left her frustrated and tense. She enjoyed the warmth and intimacy of their bodily contact yet wondered whether she wasn't also supposed to feel the kind of physical ecstasy her husband obviously enjoyed.

It has crossed her mind more than once that perhaps she ought to mention her dissatisfaction to Mark. She hasn't done so, however, for fear of giving him the impression that he is sexually inadequate. Lately she finds herself more and more irritated over things that didn't used to bother her. When she and Mark get into an argument— often shouting at each other furiously–they both end up withdrawing, sulking in silence for hours.

Can you explain what has happened to Joan and Mark? What, if anything, has either of them done wrong? Are they just sexually incompatible? What would you advise them to do? Who might be able to help them?

Quite aside from the obvious anatomical distinctions between men and women, in a sexual sense they function and perceive differently, too. Contrasted with their mental growth and general maturation, adolescent males begin to function sexually at an earlier age than females, probably reaching their peak of physical sex capacity in their late teens. Girls do not achieve this peak until five or even

ten years later. This has important implications both for dating and for the early years of many marriages. Most males are more speedily and directly aroused to sexual excitement than are females. The sight of a shapely woman, casual physical contact with her, a photograph of a nude or seminude, even the very thought of sex, often produces an erection almost at once.

Most men are exhausted and satisfied after a single orgasm, requiring at least a half hour–sometimes considerably longer–before they are able to repeat. Some women are capable of enjoying multiple orgasms in quick succession. This does not mean they are oversexed. The term *nymphomaniac* refers to a female who is sexually insatiable, who cannot be satisfied no matter how many sexual experiences she has. This is a very rare condition; because a woman can enjoy several orgasms in succession does not mean she is a nymphomaniac or in any other way abnormal. Neither does it cast any suspicion of inadequacy upon a woman who is content with a single orgasm. Both can be normal.

The gap in arousal time between males and females accounts for more than a few clumsy situations on dates. It is extremely important for males and females to understand each other's anatomy and physiology if they are to avoid embarrassment. This applies especially to females who may unwittingly do or say something that comes through to their dates quite different from what they intended.

This does not mean that females are less sexual than males; when aroused, they can want, need, and enjoy sex just as much as males. The point here is that they reach this stage more slowly and indirectly. Very few females are excited, for example, by the kind of photograph that can so immediately affect a male. Females are more likely to start with a more generalized feeling of emotional warmth and romance, moving slowly from that to a more specific desire for sex.

In contrast to males who ordinarily require very little preparation before intercourse, most females need to be introduced to coitus through what is commonly called foreplay–that is, affection, kissing, fondling, and petting. Males who overlook this difference, who proceed to intercourse at their own natural pace without considering the condition or needs of their partners, do not share a mutually satisfactory sexual experience.

Note, though, that there are differences even within differences.

A minority of females are aroused and excited sexually as rapidly and directly as males. There is no such thing as a rigid standard of normality branding as neurotic anyone who differs from it.

A MATTER OF TIMING A woman is more likely than a man to enjoy, even to require, a general feeling of personal warmth, coziness, being held closely and affectionately, being cuddled–at first without any explicit sexual intention. Even after such an interlude of affection has led to a more directly sexual approach, she needs more time than her male partner to be ready for intercourse. There is a physiological basis for this: as already noted, her vagina becomes enlarged and lubricated at a slower pace than a male's penis expands and stiffens.

Each of us must be sensitive to our partner's nature and timing. The road to successful sex is one of mutuality. In a relationship it often takes a good deal of patient experimentation before two partners can adjust to each other's preferences and timing. Such delicate accommodation is impossible in casual, transitory sexual encounters. This is one of several reasons why prostitutes seldom achieve orgasms and so many female teenagers find their first attempts at intercourse to be bitterly disappointing.

While males are more likely to be the "aggressors," it is not always or necessarily so. A Harvard psychiatrist has told me that with increasing frequency he finds females to be the initiators of sexual encounters on the campus. This is likely to be truer on the college than on the high school level, but it can happen at any age. Not only are there females who mislead their dates innocently but also there are those who may do so intentionally, trying to see how far they can encourage males to go before deliberately, sadistically stopping them. Quite probably women who do this hate men and need to demonstrate how much power they can wield over them. Whatever their motive, this kind of teasing is dangerous and terribly unfair. A primary requisite for healthy relationships between men and women–indeed, for all people generally–is that each one must understand, accept, and respect the other.

This recalls to mind the problem of Joan and Mark who began this chapter. Mark apparently failed to realize how important it is for both partners to reach orgasm during intercourse. A woman who becomes sexually excited but is left persistently unfulfilled may suffer severe nervous tension or even develop an aversion to sexual intercourse. Some couples believe simultaneous orgasms represent the ultimate in sexual success. This, however, is very difficult to achieve; seldom can the tactics and timing of two sexually excited individuals be so perfectly coordinated that they *come* at precisely the same instant. When, as is usually the case, the man tends to reach his climax first, he must then be sure his partner achieves similar satisfaction. If his penis, after orgasm, has softened, he can then fondle the female's clitoris with his fingers until she, too, *comes.* Some women, in fact, reach an even higher level of satisfaction and pleasure this way than through clitoral stimulation by the penis.

*D*ON'T BE BASHFUL! There is almost no sexual problem that cannot be solved if faced honestly and with competent help. There are many that can become bothersome if allowed to fester without adequate help. For this reason I would encourage you to discuss whatever problems of this kind you may have with an older person. It does little good to talk about them only to others your own age. Those who talk loudest and boldest are seldom the ones who really know the most.

*W*HAT IS A MAN? WHAT IS A WOMAN? You may already have discovered that adolescence can be simultaneously a painfully agonizing and ecstatically happy time of life. More than any other stage of human development, it is marked by an intense search for identity. During these years you know that you are no longer a child, yet you sometimes wonder whether you are really an adult. On the same day—within a single hour!—you may behave in ways both patently childish and amazingly adult. A large part of this quest for identity is your urgent need to become not only an adult generally but a man or woman specifically.

A sixteen-year-old young woman has described this exciting yet tumultuous time of life as follows:

> Every day, just about, something new seems to be happening to this body of mine, and I get scared sometimes. . . . I think of my two best friends, and how their faces are all broken out, and I worry mine will break out, too, but so far it hasn't, and I think of my sizes, and I

can't get it out of my head–the chest size and the stomach size and what I'll be wearing and whether I'll be able to fit into this kind of dress or the latest swimsuit. Well, it goes on and on, and I'm dizzy. . . .

Everything is growing and changing. I can see my mother watching me. I can see everyone watching me. There are times when I think I see people watching me when they really couldn't care less! . . . I wish a lot of the time I could just go back to being a little girl, without all these problems and these decisions.

My brother isn't doing too good, either. He's got acne, and he can't shave without hurting himself because of those pimples. He doesn't like an electric shaver; he says they don't feel clean to his face. He's a nut about taking showers. Two a day. He's always using deodorant. He's got all that hair under his arms. So do I. We will have our "buddy talks," and a lot of the time we just ask "When will it end?–so we can just have a body that looks the same from one week to the other."

We're in this together, my brother and me, and my friends. That's what I think about in the night–how we're all sweating it out, including my parents and my little sister. It used to be my brother and I ran around naked, or almost naked, but now I don't even look at my own bottom; I just get into a state, wondering and realizing how much has happened to me down there, so fast.[1]

*W*HAT IS A MAN? What or who is a man? Many males mistakenly suppose the answer is one of sexual prowess. The larger a male's penis, the stronger his sexual desires, the more frequently he indulges in intercourse, and the greater the number of his partners–the more manly he is. Right?

Wrong! Quite the contrary: The more compulsively a human male needs to "make" every attractive person he sees, the less probable it is that he is really a man. In all likelihood he is trying to compensate for a gnawing sense of uncertainty and insecurity. Such a person may succeed in demonstrating he is a sexual athlete; this, however, is by no means the same as being a man.

You most probably remember the biblical story of Joseph and Potiphar's wife. Joseph, having been sold by his jealous brothers into slavery and brought by his masters into Egypt, has become chief steward in the household of an Egyptian official named Potiphar. We read in Genesis 39:7-20:

After a time, his master's wife cast her eyes upon Joseph and said, "Lie with me." But he refused. He said to his master's wife, "Look, with me here, my master gives no thought to anything in his house and all that he owns he has placed in my hands. He wields no more authority in this house than I, and he has withheld nothing from me except yourself, since you are his wife. How then could I do this most wicked thing and sin before God?" And much as she coaxed Joseph day after day, he did not yield to her request to lie beside her, to be with her.

Potiphar's wife eventually tried to force herself on Joseph. When he continued to reject her advances, she denounced Joseph to her husband, falsely claiming that he had tried to rape her. Believing his wife, Potiphar had Joseph imprisoned.

Why did Joseph refuse to have intercourse with his master's wife? Was it because he was afraid of sex? Would he have been more a man had he yielded and gone to bed with her? Is it manly to reject a woman's sexual advances? Was Potiphar's wife more a woman because of her strong feeling for Joseph and her desire to have intercourse with him?

*W*HAT IS A WOMAN? The question "What is a woman?" brings us to the other side of our inquiry. Much of what has already been suggested applies here, too. It is a grotesque mistake to suppose that the more males a female can attract and seduce the more womanly she is. Certainly sex has something to do with being a man or a woman. *Something*—but not *everything*. It is the total person that qualifies as man or woman not just genitals.

It is easier to say what manliness or womanliness is not than what it is. Perhaps the best way to approach a positive answer would be by referring back to the criteria of maturity previously traced. A person who has done reasonably well in meeting these standards and who sees and uses his or her sexuality not as the be-all and end-all in itself but as one important part of a whole personality is well on the way toward being a man or woman.

Such a person understands two additional important truths about sex: (1) It is one of the most important drives in human experience; as such, it cannot successfully be denied or repressed, nor can it be turned on and off at will. And (2) the sex part of us is intimately related to every other part, especially to our emotions. The way we feel about life in general and the opposite sex in particular has much to do with our specific sex behavior. The opposite is equally true. How we act sexually affects our emotions and our attitudes toward life and other people. In short, sex is not a segment or compartment of our being. It is a strong impulse, part of our very essence, which is inseparably related to everything we are or do.

It takes more than a stiff penis to make a man. No human male erection can equal that of a chimpanzee or bull. What distinguishes human from animal sexuality is not quantity or size but quality and love.

It takes more than an enlarged vagina and multiple orgasms to make a woman. Womanly success is measured not by the number of males she can entice but by the depth of commitment and genuine love that moves her to copulate with a man who is, for her, different from all other men.

*W*HAT DO YOU THINK? The education committee of the temple was meeting to discuss a course in marriage preparation the rabbi proposed to give to juniors and seniors of the high school department. This book was to be the text; each member of the committee had been provided with a copy in advance, and they all had read it.

While most members of the committee were enthusiastically in favor of the course and thanked the rabbi for his suggestion that it be given, some had serious misgivings. One said, for example: "I'm not a prude, but I must admit that certain pages of this book embarrassed me; I wouldn't want my seventeen-year-old daughter to read them. It's all right to give our high school youngsters sex information in general, but I don't approve of going into such minute detail. The diagrams especially bothered me. Can't we leave anything to the imagination?"

"I agree," another member said eagerly. "What bothers me even more is the information given about birth control. Don't you think it's time enough for young people to learn about such things when they are ready for marriage? I don't mind telling you I'm even worried a little that this kind of information may encourage some of our boys and girls to go further sexually than they otherwise would."

This last comment evoked vigorous disagreement from one

woman on the committee. "Oh, no," she exclaimed, "how can you even think such a thing? Our boys and girls come from decent, ethical homes, where they have been taught the difference between right and wrong. I can't believe that any of them would violate the sex ethics they have been taught by their parents. As a matter of fact, my objection to this course is that sex education belongs in the home not in the religious school. We shouldn't usurp the rights of parents."

"I don't agree with any of these objections," said the newest member of the committee. "I like the idea of the course and I approve the book. My only suggestion would be that certain chapters or parts of them should be taught separately to boys and girls. I think, for example, that if the diagrams and discussions on the male and female sex organs were covered in separate groups–with the rabbi teaching the boys and a female physician or nurse instructing the girls–there would be less embarrassment. Otherwise, I'm all for it!"

What would your reactions be if you were on this committee? Would you have voted for or against the course? Why? How would you have responded to each of the arguments summarized above? Are there other objections that could have been voiced at this meeting? Has any part of this book thus far embarrassed you?

NOTES
GENDER DIFFERENCES
1. R. Coles and G. Stokes, *Sex and the American Teenager* (New York: Harper & Row, 1985), pp. 2ff.

"IF NOT NOW, WHEN?"

Since Steven entered college and joined a fraternity, he has found himself deeply troubled over ideas about sex he had previously taken for granted. Judging from the conversations of his fraternity brothers, he seemed to be just about the only one in the house who was still celibate.

The young biology instructor to whom he had gone for advice encouraged him to experience intercourse. "It isn't natural," he said, "to repress your sexual urges. Wherever we look in the animal kingdom, we see that the young male begins to have intercourse as soon as he is biologically ready for it. After all we human beings are animals, too. We can't fight nature, and the need to satisfy our sexual desires is a part of nature. A man who doesn't have intercourse before marriage builds up so strong a sex need that his wife will never be able to satisfy him. As a result he is less likely to remain faithful after marriage than if he had indulged. So my advice to you is to stop trying to be the exception that proves the rule."

How good was this advice? Why? Was the instructor correct in his comparison of men and animals? Is it true that satisfaction of our sexual desires is a part of nature? Were any factors of importance omitted by the instructor? Is it true that abstinence before marriage decreases the probability of faithfulness after marriage?

You may recognize the title of this chapter from Rabbi Hillel's famous queries: "If I am not for myself, who will be for me? If I am only for myself, what am I? And if not now, when?" I am reasonably sure Hillel did not have sex in mind when he asked these questions. Yet you might well use his words in facing questions of sex yourself.

$\mathscr{S}$OME STATISTICS A 1978 survey reported that by age eighteen 56 percent of males and 44 percent of females had experienced intercourse at least once. According to another study, the percentage of teenage girls who had intercourse by their nineteenth birthday increased from 30 percent in 1971 to 43 percent in 1976 and to 50 percent in 1986.[1]

Sociologist Nancy Clatworthy of Ohio State University found a declining trend: the rate of premarital intercourse among female college students dropped from 80 percent in 1975 to 50 percent by 1980.[2] Dr. Bernard Murstein at Connecticut College has reported similar findings on sexual intercourse by age sixteen:

	1979	1989
Males	70 percent	43 percent
Females	66 percent	20 percent[3]

While part of this reversal can be attributed to fear of herpes and AIDS, there may be other causes involved as well, which we shall consider shortly.

$\mathscr{W}$HO DOES IT? What characterizes young people who are most likely to engage in sexual intercourse at an early age? The following chart shows the relationship between sexual activity and academic ambition:

Those who expect to . . .	% who have had intercourse
Finish only some high school	78
Finish all of high school	39
Finish some college	27
Finish all of college	24
Attend a graduate school	23[4]

A 1986 survey by Louis Harris discloses similar findings for both sexes between the ages of twelve and seventeen:

Grade averages	% who have had intercourse
Between C and F	37
B- to B	25
B+ to A	21[5]

A group called Educational Communications of Illinois ques-
tioned top-level high school students–that is, those listed in *Who's
Who among American High School Students*. Seventy-six percent
reported they had not had intercourse. Only 8 percent favored
unmarried couples' living together.[6]

Clearly there is a significant correlation between academic
achievement and early premarital sexual activity. A similar connection involves the marital happiness of a teenager's parents.

Marital status of parents	% of adolescents who have had intercourse
Divorced	49
Separated	40
Married	26[7]

What is the correlation of teenage sexual behavior and the
amount of communication on the subject with a parent? A sixteen-
year-old girl has expressed herself on this most movingly:

> But then sex gets going, and I lose my control, and so does the guy,
> and it's as if we're trying to find one thing and we get so excited, we
> get lost. Then, who do you turn to–if you want to stop and think
> about where you're headed? Your parents are away, or they're too
> busy; the minister (at least ours) preaches at you, and I just feel so
> bad after he gets through listing my sins. The teachers aren't the
> ones–that sex-education course is a joke, and the guy who gives it is
> another joke. There's no one![8]

This teenager isn't the only one to feel as she did. Of the many
young people studied in the *Rolling Stone* survey already cited, only
36 percent said they could seek sexual information from their parents; 47 percent, by contrast, would ask their friends, siblings, or
sex partners. Two-thirds of the females who reported they could not
discuss sex with their mothers were no longer virgins.[9]

The evidence is clear. The young person who possesses self-
esteem, academic ambition, high intelligence, long-range goals, a
sense of purpose–whose parents are still married and who can easily
talk to at least one of them about sex–is far more likely to be virginal
or celibate than the one who lacks these characteristics.

*W*HY DO THEY DO IT? The first, most immediate, most obvious answer to this question is that "they" feel the mounting pressure of sexual desire, which "they" are unwilling or unable to suppress. As is so often true in trying to explain human behavior, however, the quickest, easiest response is usually only superficial: in the previous cases other, unconscious, more fundamental needs were also being satisfied.

When asked directly why they had initiated sexual intercourse, a group of high school students gave the following conscious reasons: for fun, to get it over with, to fit in with the crowd, curiosity, to avoid breaking up with a dating partner, as a way of getting love, for money, because they were unable to exercise self-control, because it felt good, because everyone else was doing it, because they were ready to share their body with someone else.[10]

Which of these do you think are sound reasons? Which are not sound? Can you think of better reasons, not included on this list?

A physician who specializes in sexual problems gives us further insight into the deeper drives that often propel adolescents to undertake premarital intercourse. Dr. Louis L. Fine asserts: "The sexual act of a young adolescent is not, in most instances, one of erotic or physical pleasure. Nonsexual motivations—be they to gain peer approval, to escape from home, to rebel against parents, to express hostility, to search (vainly) for love, to compensate for depression, or to signal for help—are the most frequent underlying reasons for sexual behavior."[11]

You may already have discovered that peer pressure toward intercourse can seem almost irresistible. The next time a friend tries to push you in this direction, you might ask yourself such questions as: What purpose can he/she possibly be trying to achieve? What difference could it really make to her/him whether I do or do not have intercourse (unless, of course, the person trying to persuade you wants you to have intercourse with him/her)? Is this friend just trying to assuage his/her own guilt or insecurity by inducing others to do the same thing?

*R*EBELLING AGAINST A REBELLION? Intercourse as an expression of real love is a wholesome, ecstatic, sacred experience. Intercourse as a substitute or search for real love, as a frantic protest against adolescent insecurity or adult domination, is self-destructive.

The realization of this truth by some who began having intercourse for the wrong reasons is, in addition to the fear of disease, another cause of the apparent decrease in the rate of teenage intercourse. In 1980 *Cosmopolitan* magazine surveyed more than 106,000 women on their sexual attitudes and behavior. The editors concluded: "So many readers wrote negatively about the sexual revolution, expressing longings for vanished intimacy, and the now elusive joys of romance and commitment, that we began to sense that there might be a sexual counterrevolution under way in America."[12] To some extent these reactions may be the result of extreme disappointment some individuals–especially females–experience with their first intercourse. In their major series of interviews–perhaps the most important ever of this kind–Drs. Coles and Stokes learned that 35 percent of the males they studied and 72 percent of the females reported their postcoital feelings as *sorry* or *ambivalent* rather than *glad.*[13]

Dr. George Leonard, who has written extensively on sex, approaches the root of the matter when he writes: "Casual recreational sex is hardly a feast–not even a good, hearty sandwich. It is a diet of fast food served in plastic containers. Life's feast is available only to those who are willing and able to engage life on a deeply personal level. . . ."[14]

Rolling Stone magazine, which sponsored the study by Drs. Cole and Stokes, also asked adults, most of whom had themselves engaged in premarital intercourse, how they now felt about their earlier experiences and what advice they would give to their own adolescents. Ellen Goodman, the well-known columnist, summarizes their responses thus: "When asked whether the permissive attitudes toward sex–*their* generation's attitudes towards sex–were a change for the better or for the worse, a full 59 percent of all respondents said this change was for the worse. . . ."[15]

*Y*OU'RE THE BOSS The decision about when to have your first sexual intercourse, or whether or not to "go all the way" before you marry, is strictly yours to make. It is important that you shape a firm policy in advance, then govern your daily decisions accordingly rather than just act spontaneously so that a whole series of nondecisions becomes a policy after all.

A good marriage may be one of the most important destinations you will ever have. Though it may still seem remote to you, it is essential that you begin to decide now what kind of marriage you

would like to have, the quality of sex life you want in it, and the steps to be taken during the intervening years if you are to succeed. Whatever your decision regarding premarital sexual intercourse, it should be made after the most careful consideration of all relevant facts, of all the options available to you, and the probable consequences of each.

Aaron agrees there is no justification for a double standard in sex behavior. He contends that the single standard for both genders should be permissive, that is to say, both males and females should feel free to enjoy whatever sex affairs they desire before marriage. He has, as a matter of fact, been urging this freedom on his current girlfriend. He says that, despite the absence of real love between them, they both feel physically aroused when they are together, and he sees no reason why they should abstain from meeting each other's needs.

Since neither had had sexual intercourse before, there need be no fear of disease. Since they are both intelligent college students, they should be able to prevent pregnancy. He concedes readily that the two of them do not have enough in common for marriage, but to him this is no reason they shouldn't give each other pleasure now in the one area they do seem to share.

How intelligent is Aaron's attitude? What are some of the possible or probable consequences if his advice is followed? What effect would following his suggestion have on a future marriage of either to someone else?

Despite my efforts thus far to be nonjudgmental and objective, you are no doubt already aware that in your decision on when to start experiencing sexual intercourse I opt for later, not now. It wouldn't be fair to expand on my view, though, without first summarizing the opinions of those who disagree with me.

Advocates of premarital intercourse say, first, that economic factors in today's society necessitate the delay of marriage far beyond the age of sexual maturity, making it unrealistic to expect that most people will delay intercourse until marriage.

Their next argument is that, since sexual compatibility is so important in marriage, like other essential factors this, too, should be tested before a long-lasting commitment is made.

Third, the correct causal connection between sex and love is acknowledged by many of those who favor premarital intercourse. But they say that a ceremony and license do not really determine the quality of that relationship. In the words of sociologist Judith Fales: "It is possible for an unmarried couple to show more mutual concern and care than a married couple."

Finally, proponents of sexual intercourse before marriage remind us that in the past some couples have entered into unsuccessful marriages because they found the sexual demands irresistible and had been taught that it is wrong to have intercourse outside the sanctions of wedlock.

Without for a moment denying some measure of truth in these claims, let me here state more explicitly what I have already implied: on balance I strongly recommend, especially for young people your age, abstinence from intercourse until later.

MY OWN VIEW The heart of my argument is the vital, dynamic relationship between sex and love, on which I have already quoted the eloquent words of Rabbi Borowitz and Dr. Fromm. The pervasive mood of American society today is oblivious to, even contemptuous of, this relationship. Dr. George Leonard offers intriguing evidence: Several years ago he attended a weekend retreat for sexologists held at the Institute for Advanced Study of Human Sexuality, a self-proclaimed graduate school in San Francisco. He was shocked that throughout the entire program of intensive observation and discussion the word *love* wasn't mentioned even once! He summarizes his entire experience thus: "Nothing was shocking, but nothing was sacred either." To this he adds: "As for 'sex,' it has become something you 'have.' You have a car, you have dinner, you have a swim, you have the chicken pox . . . and you have sex." Dr. Leonard then urges us not to "equate a powerful urge, an intimate relationship, an act that can transform the human body and lead to the creation of life, with a commodity, a meal, an exercise, and a disease." I do not doubt the possibility of some unmarried couples' possessing keener sexual sensitivity than some married couples. Yet the odds are very much against such exceptions. The younger the people involved, the truer this becomes. With individuals of high school or early college age the great danger in accepting love as a criterion for intercourse is the likelihood of confusing infatuation with love. Then the question arises as to the number of partners with whom one can experience intercourse on what one honestly believes at the moment to be the level of love, only to discover later that it wasn't love at all. How many partners will it take to blunt the sensitive, delicate connection between coitus and love?

Drs. Coles and Stokes put it this way: "In the absence of notions like commitment and responsibility, hormones can look an awful lot like 'love.'" Perhaps this is one reason it has been reported that only 14 percent of the relationships between teenagers who have had intercourse last more than a year.

How do you decide if you're ready for sex? In her "ASK BETH" column in *The Boston Globe*, August 9, 1990, in the piece "Sense about Sex," Beth Winship provides some sage advice:

> You aren't ready when you feel worried, uncertain, or scared. Many people don't think intercourse is right until they are married or in a fully committed, loving, and mature relationship. You must search your own mind, including your family's values, to discover what you really think. Answering the following questions will help you clarify your thoughts:
>
> Are you really knowledgeable about sexuality for both males and females? Ignorance can make this experience risky and full of unpleasant surprises.
>
> Do you know about reliable birth control measures? Where to get them? Have you the courage to ask for them? Will you surely use them?
>
> Do you and your partner intend to have him use condoms? Can you talk about this together?
>
> Do you accept responsibility for possible consequences, such as pregnancy or a sexually transmitted disease? Do you know where to get help?
>
> Is your relationship committed? Are you mutually understanding and considerate of each other?
>
> Are you mature enough emotionally to be this intimate? Can you discuss your feelings? In intercourse you surrender your individuality for mutual intimacy. Do you have enough self-confidence to be this vulnerable?
>
> Are your motives for having sex pleasure and closeness? Or do you feel you must to please your boyfriend or try to keep him or prove you're adult? These aren't good reasons for having intercourse.
>
> Again, do you really approve of this for yourself morally? Lingering guilt spoils many an early sexual experience. It takes considerable maturity to search your own mind and know truthfully what you believe. Remember, there are ways other than intercourse to show affection and intimacy.

Isn't it possible to experience intercourse on a purely physical level at first, without love or commitment, then to transpose it after marriage to a higher, more mature dimension? Theoretically, yes; in reality, very questionable. The more a person has indulged in intercourse just for pleasure or release and the greater the number of his or her sexual partners, the less likely is later transposition to a superior dimension.

An analogy may be helpful here. The eye is an extremely sensitive organ, able to distinguish among minute shadings of color. Were we to ignore this fact, to expose our eyes persistently and without protection to brightest sunshine, perhaps even to stare directly at an eclipse of the sun, we would soon destroy the exquisite sensitivity of our eyes. I am convinced that in much the same manner a man or woman who chooses to experience intercourse on less than the highest sensitivity level of which he or she is innately capable will, after a time, damage or even destroy that capacity.

The argument that sexual compatibility should be tested before marriage, which at first sounds so logical and reasonable, falls flat on its face. It isolates sex from all other aspects of marital relationship. Only rarely do couples meet with instantaneously mutual success sexually. A man and woman who are committed to a permanent partnership on many levels can gradually work toward improving their sexual lives. Where both permanence and commitment are lacking, two pitfalls loom. Immediate sexual success can convince the pair they are right for each other when in fact they are not. Or initial disappointment in sex can encourage them to break off when they might in the course of time have achieved an excellent sexual adjustment through patience and love.

*T*RIAL RUN It is quite common these days for couples to live together before marrying. You yourself may know such couples. If the views of those who favor premarital intercourse were entirely valid, we should expect—should we not?—that such couples would achieve greater success in their marriages than others. Yet this is clearly not so. Research reported in mid-1989, covering many thousands of individuals, indicates that among those who have lived together before marrying the rate of divorce within ten years of their wedding is 38 percent. This compares with 27 percent for those who did not cohabit!

$\mathscr{S}$UMMING UP Whether or not you follow my advice on premarital intercourse, two types of behavior are inexcusable. The first is that of a male who takes advantage of a female by claiming "love" as a reason to have intercourse. When Planned Parenthood in Chicago asked a thousand young men whether they considered it acceptable to lie by telling a young woman they loved her in order to persuade her to have intercourse, 70 percent said *yes*! It shouldn't be necessary for me to comment on the gross immorality of such an attitude.

It is no less reprehensible for an unmarried couple to have intercourse without using effective contraception. If only their own interpersonal relationship were at stake, that would be simpler. Far worse is the inestimable damage that can be done to an innocent child who did not ask to be born and who was unwanted.

Few types of human behavior are more unforgivable than that of a male who impregnates a female, then tries to deny or evade his obligations. Any male who undertakes intercourse before marriage must do all in his power to prevent pregnancy; if it occurs nonetheless, he must share with his partner the decisions and responsibilities that ensue.

Because sexuality is so sensitive and significant in our lives, no analogy to other types of human experience can be more than partially instructive. Perhaps eating comes closer than any other. You can, if you wish, guzzle your food gluttonously, with regard for neither neatness nor manners. Or you can dine at a well-set table by candlelight with a special someone, enjoying his or her company and conversation while eating. Better yet, you can add a tone of sanctity to your meal by starting it with an expression of gratitude to God for your food, praying that this gesture may enhance your spiritual as well as your physical nourishment. Best of all, you can sit at a סֵדֶר *seder* table, inviting your food to reinvigorate your relationship with the Jewish people, with all who struggle for freedom, and with God.

Where this analogy is lacking is that you can alter your table manners at will. Your sexual inclinations and associations, once established, are much harder to change.

Judaism excels in recognizing the intensely important relationship between sex and love. It is clearly more than a verbal coincidence that the verb used in the Torah for intercourse is יָדַע *yada*, meaning "knew." Thus we read in Genesis 4:1: "And the man knew

Eve his wife; and she conceived and bore Cain. . . ." Our faith teaches that intercourse at its best was intended by God and nature to be much more than just physical gratification, as important as that undeniably is. It should involve two people *knowing* each other, respecting and caring for each other deeply in both physical and spiritual dimensions, loving each other enough to seek a permanent sharing of their lives and the creation of new life.

*J*UDAISM YESTERDAY   What does Judaism teach about premarital intercourse? It will probably surprise, perhaps even shock, you to learn that nowhere in either the Bible or the Talmud is there an explicit prohibition of intercourse before marriage. This does not mean ancient Judaism condoned premarital intercourse. The absence of a direct law on this matter can be understood only in the larger context of social conditions prevailing among Jews at that time. We must remember marriage took place at a much earlier age then and was often arranged by parents when the prospective bride and groom were young children. Most couples were wedded in their late teens after a full year of betrothal. With betrothal in the mid-teens and marriage a year later, what need was there for laws prohibiting premarital intercourse?

Because of eroding communal standards in medieval times, and because couples were no longer betrothed and married at so young an age, it became necessary for the first time that Jewish law prohibit premarital intercourse explicitly as it had implicitly through the centuries. Maimonides included such a provision in his מִשְׁנֶה תּוֹרָה *Mishneh Torah*, the great twelfth-century legal code.

The definitive judgment of traditional Judaism on this matter has been summarized as follows:

> Chastity before marriage has been considered an obvious requirement for all and was taken for granted by the tradition. . . . There are many statements that support this point of view and demand that an unmarried person refrain from sexual intercourse. The references deal particularly with males (*Pes.* 113a, b; *Shab.* 152a). A statement of Rabbi Yochanan makes this very clear: "There is a small organ in man; he who satisfies it goes hungry and he who allows it to go hungry is satisfied" (*San.* 107a). . . . All females were expected to be virgins at the time of their first marriage. The dowry of a nonvirgin was less than that of a virgin, and anyone falsely claiming virginity was subject to severe punishment.[16]

Why are these talmudic statements addressed particularly to males? Does this indicate that celibacy in men was considered more important than virginity in women? Express in your own words what Rabbi Yochanan was trying to say? Do you agree?

*J*UDAISM TODAY Rabbi Eugene Borowitz has done an excellent job of expanding on the traditional opinion, transposing it into modern terms directly applicable to your life:[17] He has clearly described the various levels on which two individuals can have intercourse. With only minor modifications I intend to relate his pattern here. For reasons that will become apparent as we proceed, these levels will be numbered in reverse.

Level five is that of conquest or force. This kind of conduct is rape. Women have organized in recent years to advise one another on how to avoid or resist being raped, offering compassionate guidance and help to those who have been thus victimized. To the rapist, sex is only an instrument of power, a way of imposing himself and his will on someone weaker, a vain attempt to simulate self-confidence.

It is especially with reference to rape that the term "making love" is so transparently inaccurate. At its best, intercourse is a manifestation of love. But it can also indicate hate, fear, insecurity, or a variety of other emotions far removed from love.

Incest (sexual intercourse between members of an immediate family, such as between two siblings or between parent and child) and child abuse must also be classified on level five. Victims of sexual abuse, whether they remember it or have repressed it in the subconscious as experience too painful to be endured, can nearly always be helped by wise and patient counseling. Teachers, rabbis, physicians, psychologists, and psychiatrists are among those who can help them.

Level four is that of the "healthy orgasm." This level emerges from a perception of our sexuality as a strong physiological need that is healthy to express, unwholesome to repress. The underlying assumption or code is simple: When hungry, we eat; when thirsty, we drink; when afflicted with an itch, we scratch; when desirous of sex, we seek intercourse.

Is it true that it may be harmful to one's health to frustrate so intense a natural urge as sex? If that meant total and absolute repression–no release of sexual tension even through masturbation or petting–the answer would probably be yes.

Yet we should remember that premarital intercourse at an early age may also involve serious physical or emotional risk to one's health. Dr. Elizabeth Whelan writes:

> There is now increasing evidence that some of the emotional side effects of a premature permissive sexual relationship may have long-range effects on the development of personality, damaging a person's emotional stability.[18]

Dr. Whelan cites specific studies to support her view, then continues:

> Statistics have shown that girls who begin to have intercourse early in their life (roughly, before the age of sixteen) are twice as likely to develop cancer of the cervix than are those girls who delay intercourse until some time in their twenties.[19]

Level three is that of "mutual consent." Where level five definitely and level four probably exemplify the desire of an individual to fulfill his or her own sexual needs, the partner being only a means to that end, here on level three we come to consideration for both participants. Two people feel a desire for sex at the same time. Finding each other to be physically attractive, they agree to satisfy their mutual need. Neither is imposing anything upon the other or taking advantage of the other. Instead of one individual seeking a healthy orgasm, two agree to do so mutually and simultaneously.

*C*ONFUSING CAUSE AND EFFECT *Level two is that of love.* For the first time intercourse becomes part of a relationship between two whole personalities, not just two genital systems. As one competent observer has commented: "Penises and vaginas can't love each other; only people can do that." Intercourse as an expression of love reverses what some people believe to be the relationship between the two. Very often the assumption is that first two individuals are sexually attracted, then they enjoy successful intercourse, which increases the attraction, and finally this leads to love. Without denying that perhaps this does occasionally take place, many experts in the field of marriage feel the opposite is truer: that is, first two people who are initially attracted to each other deepen their relationship as human beings to the point of love, after which they express this love, among other ways, by sharing intercourse. Renowned psychoanalyst Erich Fromm has expressed this concept as well as anyone. He rejects "the notion that mutual sexual satisfaction was supposed to be the basis for satisfactory love relations and especially for a happy marriage." Dr. Fromm assures us that the opposite is true:

> The underlying idea was that love is the child of sexual pleasure and that, if two people learn how to satisfy each other sexually, they will love each other. . . . One ignored the fact that the contrary of the underlying assumption is true. Love is not the result of adequate sexual satisfaction, but sexual happiness–even the knowledge of the so-called sexual technique–is the result of love.[20]

Those who advocate that intercourse be restricted to love say that various types of human behavior are appropriate to different degrees of relationships. One politely nods toward a casual acquaintance, shakes hands with a person to whom he or she has just been introduced, affectionately hugs an old friend, passionately kisses a mate. To shower a casual or new acquaintance with hugs and kisses would be highly questionable if not comic behavior. The question, then, is: At what degree in the relationship between two persons is sexual intercourse appropriate? The answer, for those who take their stand here, is: on the level of love, not before.

Level one is that of reserving intercourse for marriage. It is easy, under the persistent urging of sexual desire, to confuse love with infatuation. A psychiatrist has quoted a young female patient of his as saying: "I believe one should have intercourse only when in love, so I am constantly in love." Without being quite so ridiculous or bold as that, many individuals act on a similar premise. Adherents of level one remind us of the time test we used previously to distinguish love from infatuation. To this they would add that there is a difference between "love for now" and "love forever." When two people not only feel the strongest kind of interpersonal relationship but are ready on that basis to commit themselves to each other, to assume what they hope will be permanent responsibility for each other, then intercourse between them becomes appropriate and proper.

*W*HAT DO YOU THINK? Gabe has had intercourse with several young women. Though he acknowledges that he has loved none of them, he is satisfied that he has done the right thing. "I'm sure," he has said, "that it's better for me to have this experience now before I marry. Otherwise, how would I know what intercourse is supposed to be like or whether what I have with my wife is really good? I'll now have a basis for comparison."

How valid is Gabe's argument? Suppose, based on the kind of comparison he mentions, he decides later that his sex life with his wife isn't as enjoyable as his earlier experiences? With how many females would he have to do this in order to be sure?

NOTES
"IF NOT NOW, WHEN?"
1. C. Cassell, *Straight from the Heart* (New York: Simon & Schuster, 1987), p. 110.
2. *The New York Times*, October 4, 1983.
3. *Vitality Digest*, June 1989.
4. R. Coles and G. Stokes, *Sex and the American Teenager* (New York: Harper & Row, 1985), p. 78.
5. *Phi Delta Kappa*, June 1987.
6. S. and J. Gordon, *Raising a Child Conservatively in a Sexually Permissive World* (New York: Simon & Schuster, 1983), p. 102.
7. Coles and Stokes, *Sex and the American Teenager*, p. 77.
8. *Ibid.*, p. 10.
9. *Ibid.*, pp. 36, 99.
10. C. Cassell, *Straight from the Heart*, p. 89.
11. *Ibid.*, p. 112.
12. *Cosmopolitan*, September 1980.
13. Coles and Stokes, *Sex and the American Teenager*, p. 73.
14. *Esquire*, December 1982.
15. *The Boston Globe*, March 29, 1988.
16. *American Reform Responsa* (New York: Central Conference of American Rabbis, 1983), p. 477.
17. E. Borowitz, *Choosing a Sex Ethic* (New York: Schocken Books, 1969).
18. *Parents* magazine, February 1975.
19. *Ibid.*
20. Erich Fromm, *The Art of Loving* (New York: Harper & Bros, 1956), pp. 88ff.

DATE OR MATE?

Do you date? If so, do you enjoy it, feel secure while doing it, look forward to further dates? If not, do you wish you could; do you feel inferior to those who date a lot; do you think dating is a waste of time?

If you consider dating to be nothing more than an evening of fun, you're mistaken. It is an opportunity to learn more about yourself as well as about various types of other people and how you relate to them. Effective and enjoyable dating is a way of getting to know and to deal with your own sexual impulses. In that respect and others it can be good preparation for eventual marriage.

What do you seek in a dating partner? What traits in another person prompt you to ask her or him for a date? Dr. Aaron Hass, an expert on teenager behavior, asked a large number of young men what qualities they sought in a female whom they wanted to date. Here, in order of importance, are their responses:

1. Good looks, good body
2. Friendly, not conceited
3. Intelligent
4. Sense of humor
5. Honest–"not into game-playing"
6. Good conversationalist
7. Similar interests and values
8. Sexually open–"not a prude, but I don't want her to have been with a lot of guys"
9. Outgoing, not shy
10. Mature–"that she have a serious side, too"

When the same question was addressed to young women, their responses came out this way:

1. Intelligent
2. Good looks, good body
3. Good conversationalist–"easy to talk to"
4. Sincere, honest–"not just out for sex"
5. Confident, but not conceited
6. Sense of humor, fun to be with
7. Clean-cut–well groomed, not into drugs or alcohol
8. Romantic/affectionate
9. Popular at school
10. Gentle–"not hung up about having to be a 'man'"

What significant differences, if any, do you find between these lists? Do they coincide with your dating preferences? To what extent do you think the traits listed here would also be valid for choosing a marriage partner?

*T*HUS FAR, NO FARTHER! The question of petting will almost inevitably arise in connection with dating. Petting serves an important purpose in nature's scheme of things. It is the prelude and preparation for coitus, nature's preface to full sexual relations, technically referred to as foreplay.

What choices do you have with regard to petting?

1. You can firmly determine to resist all temptation, never to indulge in it at all. Because your sex drive is so persistent at this age, and especially if you date one person steadily and exclusively over a long period of time, this is a highly unrealistic and improbable alternative.

2. You can "play it by ear," setting no policy in advance, just acting as the spirit and urge move you. Again, because sex can be an explosive reality, this is not wise procedure. The more actively our glands function, the more difficult it is to apply rational controls to our behavior. The middle of a raging blizzard is no time to check on whether the storm windows have been installed. Couples, therefore, should agree on a mutually acceptable policy in advance, determining how far they intend to go, then resolutely abiding by their decision.

3. A third possibility is to agree on petting but to terminate it before either partner has an orgasm. Aside from this decision requir-

ing even more self-control than not petting at all, the frustration of proceeding almost to the point of orgasm, then stopping, can be nearly intolerable. A male who has done this may actually feel physical pain in his testicles; a female may also experience pain in her groin as a consequence. In such situations a person may want to masturbate soon afterward in order to relieve the tension.

4. A couple confronting this predicament may agree to pet to the point where both of them achieve orgasm. This has the advantage of relieving tension and providing intense physical pleasure without the dangers and guilt that may be caused by proceeding to intercourse. Is there a difference of substance between intercourse and petting to orgasm? Is there such a thing as a "technical virgin," one whose partner or date has given one an orgasm but without penetration?

People will differ in their response to these questions. My own disposition is to say yes, there is a significant difference; I believe that such a person remains entitled to consider and call oneself a virgin.

*S*ELECTING A SPOUSE At the beginning of this chapter we considered the qualities most young people seek in those they date. Looking again at those lists or at your own, which of these characteristics do you think would be important for selecting not a date but a spouse? Many people who never asked themselves this question have discovered, to their great regret, that qualities they thought were attractive or cute in the short run turned out to be extremely annoying over a long period of time.

Chances are you won't be making this choice for at least several years. But your eventual success in marriage will be much more probable if you use your dating experience to judge your partners on two levels: With what type of person can you enjoy yourself for a few hours; with what type would you enjoy living in marital partnership for many years? Sometimes the two coincide—not always.

*H*OW TO JUDGE What must you look for in the selection of a mate? Much of the answer may be summed up in a single word: *compatibility.* Unfortunately, however, this is far from an easy word to define. The dictionary defines *compatible* as "capable of existing together" or "congenial." Some people have as much trouble existing together–especially in the same household–as fire and water. If this is the case, it is imperative to discover it before marriage rather than after.

Usually when a man and a woman are described as being incompatible, it is assumed they are uncongenial sexually. While this is sometimes true, there are many other kinds of compatibility on which a good marriage must depend.

1. *Intellectual compatibility.* It isn't good for a very bright man to be married to a rather dull woman, or an intelligent girl to be coupled with a stupid boy. Such a match may be exciting for a short while, but it will soon become insufferable.

2. *Social compatibility.* It isn't snobbery but rather that, undeniably, two people who come from similar social backgrounds stand a better chance for happiness in their marriage than if there is a vast gap between them in this respect. Despite all the fascinating Cinderella-type stories in print and on film, serious studies of marriage show this to be true. With similar social backgrounds it is more probable that the values and aspirations of two people will also be alike and the adjustments to be made after the wedding will be less serious than they might otherwise be.

Two people coming from widely divergent social backgrounds differ in many respects: the clothing they wear, the kinds of entertainment they enjoy, their social manners and companions, the vacations they enjoy, and so on. This doesn't mean that, given many other levels of compatibility, two such individuals can't in the course of time adjust to each other's ways, but this entails more in the list of discrepancies to which they must accommodate.

3. *Economic compatibility.* This is important, too. We have in mind here not the financial background and standing of the two families, which would actually be an aspect of social compatibility, but rather the *attitudes* and *ambitions* of bride and groom regarding financial matters. If one is a compulsive buyer and the other a habitual saver, this does not auger well–not merely because of the probable dissension between them on money matters but also because one's feelings about the saving or spending of money disclose a great deal about one's general personality.

The success of the women's liberation movement and the increase in dual career marriages add another dimension to the question of financial compatibility. A man who will feel uncomfortable about his wife's success in her career, which could be possibly more than his success in his career, has no business marrying a woman who wants very much to have a career. A woman should be as sure as possible before marrying that her prospective mate's view of women's liberation agrees with her own. Any person who retains the stereotype that a husband should in every instance be stronger and more assertive, dominant, and successful than his wife had better be sure these expectations jibe with those of a prospective mate. The same caution applies to anyone who still thinks all the responsibilities of homemaking and parenting devolve upon women. It is too late to discover discrepancies in these attitudes after your marriage has taken place.

4. *Character traits* abound in which it is important for groom and bride to be compatible. For example, if one is very rigid while the other is permissive and lax, there is probably trouble ahead. If one is punctual and the other habitually tardy, if one is neat and the other sloppy, if one is an extreme introvert and the other an enthusiastic extrovert, it is easy to anticipate some of the difficulties they almost certainly will have to face.

*M*ORE CRITERIA 5. *Cultural tastes* are of equal importance. It would be difficult for a music lover to share life meaningfully with one who hated music—or perhaps even for an opera lover to be happy with one whose musical tastes run to jazz and rock. The future would appear to be bleak if an avid reader married one who never opens a book, or a vigorous athlete were paired with a shrinking, fearful recluse, or a connoisseur of art were attracted to one who hates museums.

If opposites like those described here were sufficiently attracted to each other to enjoy dating, would that not of itself seem to indicate they have enough in common to make good marriage partners? How could we account for such individuals finding each other interesting for dating in the first place? How about the old adage "Opposites attract"?

6. *Similar leisure-time interests* bode better for marriage. Two of the earliest experts on marriage estimated that couples who share and enjoy all their outside activities together have fifteen times more chance for happiness in marriage than couples who lack such agree-

ment.[1] Would you like, incidentally, to test yourself on this with the next person you date? Pick up the current issue of any magazine or newspaper, go through it together, and find out how many items there are in which both of you are deeply interested—items about which you would like to enter upon a serious discussion.

7. *Compatibility of age* is important, too. While it is impossible to establish an exact mathematical formula, we know that too great an age disparity is not good. A woman who wishes to marry a man fifteen years her senior is apt to be unconsciously searching for a father substitute not a husband. A man in that relationship may well be anxious to find a daughter substitute rather than a wife. Similar unconscious motivations may be at work if the woman is appreciably older than the man. Marriages based on such needs are fraught with danger.

In addition to the unconscious motivations involved there are two very important practical problems to be considered when the bride is very much younger than the groom. The life expectancy of women in the United States is considerably longer than that of men. This means that, even when husband and wife are of approximately the same age, the man is likely to die first and the woman will face a certain number of years toward the end of her life as a widow. Where an age disparity exists, with the husband much older than his wife, this probability is obviously increased. While this is not a very pleasant or happy prospect to consider at the time of choosing a marriage partner, long-range possibilities must be faced in making a decision one hopes will last for life.

The other practical difficulty pertains to the future sex life of the couple. There is no reason for a woman of twenty and a man of thirty-five to face any trouble in this regard. When she is sixty, however, and he seventy-five, problems of sexual adjustment may develop.

Some men and women continue to enjoy intercourse into their seventies or even eighties, but there can be a great gap in the frequency with which a woman of sixty and a man of seventy-five desire or can repeat it.

8. *Religious compatibility* is an area whose importance would be difficult to exaggerate. This includes not only the advantage of coming from the same general religious faith but also the attitudes of the two toward religious belief and practice even when they share a common religious background.

9. *Sexual uncongeniality* does not always indicate incompatibility, though there is no denying that it sometimes does. Sex is very important in marriage–just how important depends on the age and health of the individuals involved. I very much doubt that two healthy young people can enjoy a happy marriage without a mutually satisfying and pleasurable sex life.

Sexual compatibility is likely to be a consequence not a cause of other compatibilities. Two people who are otherwise well matched and who deeply love each other–emotionally and spiritually as well as physically–will most probably achieve sexual compatibility. If they are compatible only sexually, their prospect for happiness in marriage is bleak.

*P*RIORITIES We must neither minimize nor exaggerate the importance of sex in marriage. Two of our leading experts on this subject have listed, in descending order, the ten most important ingredients of successful marriages:
1. Love, caring, and intimacy together
2. A sense of humor and playfulness
3. Honest communication and interesting conversation
4. A passionate sense of mission or purpose
5. Friends together and separately
6. Commitment to one's own identity and ideals
7. Tolerance for occasional craziness, irritableness, conflict, error
8. Acceptance of each other's style
9. Sexual fulfillment
10. Sharing household tasks

They then comment, with delightful humor underlining their seriousness:

> Occasionally, when this list is presented to an audience, an outraged male will suggest it is nonsense (no female ever has)–how could sex be number nine? The reply is always: because there are eight more important things. And besides, of the 3,243 really important aspects of a relationship, sex is one of the top ten. Not bad.[2]

What do you think of this list? Want to have a bit of fun and perhaps even learn something at the same time? Show this list to your parents and discuss it with them.

$\mathcal{P}$OSTSCRIPT Let me add here several summary comments on the general subject of compatibility. First, it would be foolish to suppose that any two people can or should be identical in all respects. Indeed, their household would likely be a dull and boring place if this were so. What is important is not that bride and groom be carbon copies of each other but that they resemble each other in most respects and do not differ too widely in the rest.

It is a dreadful mistake to marry someone with whom one knows there is serious incompatibility, in the expectation that after marriage things will change. True, two people who live lovingly in a good marriage do have an effect on each other; it has been said that sometimes husbands and wives come not only to think alike in the course of time but almost seem to resemble each other. But this is true only if there was sufficient compatibility from the outset. A home is not a reform school. If you don't love your prospective mate as he or she is, quit before you become too deeply involved.

Conversely, beware if you find no faults in your spouse-to-be. There never has been and never will be a perfect human being. If you can identify no faults, it means you don't know the other person nearly as well as you think you do. You may be sure of one thing: sooner or later after the wedding, faults will become evident–in you and in your mate. To know them in advance means to be prepared for the adjustments you will later have to make. There is another reason it is important to recognize faults in the person you intend to marry: To love means to fulfill the needs of the loved one. If you are unaware of that person's faults, how can you possibly know–far less, fulfill–his or her needs?

It is essential that you like your mate as well as love him or her, for if you do not truly like and respect a mate, it isn't love at all but at best only infatuation.

Some years ago I visited an elderly man who had lost his wife the day before. They had been married more than fifty years. As the man talked to me, he kept nodding his head sadly from side to side, saying: "Did I lose a friend! I lost the most wonderful friend a man could have!" He came eloquently close to summarizing what I am trying to convey here. If, in addition to everything else that binds them together, two people can feel they are solid friends to each other, theirs is apt to be a superb marriage.

*T*ESTING A number of tests have been devised to evaluate the personalities of two individuals who are contemplating marriage and to anticipate their probable compatibility. While no such test is infallible, and life's most important decisions cannot be made entirely on the basis of psychological evaluations, such tests can nevertheless be helpful, particularly where there is reason to doubt how well any two people are matched. We offer you here a brief chart with which two people may attempt to evaluate themselves and the relationship between them.

To be justified in considering themselves compatible, any two individuals should be much alike on at least half these items, somewhat alike on many of the rest, and without major discrepancies on more than four or five. When a dating relationship begins to grow toward permanency, it should be both interesting and instructive for you and your partner to rate yourselves by these criteria. Two steps are recommended:

1. Each of you rate your compatibility individually.
2. Compare your separate evaluations and discuss them.

The extent to which you agree can in itself be a measure of your being well matched.

HOW COMPATIBLE ARE WE?
1. Very different   3. Somewhat alike
2. Mildly different   4. Much alike

☐ Home background.
☐ Personal standards of right and wrong.
☐ Ideals regarding home and family.
☐ Desires for and feelings toward children.
☐ Educational background and interests.
☐ Intelligence.
☐ Religious interests and preferences.
☐ Vocational preferences and attitudes.
☐ Ambition for money and social standing.

☐ Spending and saving habits.
☐ Relative emphasis on home and outside activities
☐ Cultural tastes: art, music, drama, books, etc.
☐ Personal habits: eating, sleeping, smoking, etc.
☐ Circle of friends.
☐ Recreational and social interests.
☐ Temperament and mood.
☐ Punctuality and neatness.
☐ Attitudes toward parents of both.
☐ Tendency to be critical.
☐ Tendency to praise and reassure.

*M*IX AND MATCH Have your parents ever objected to your dating a non-Jew? If so, did you think they were narrow-minded or unfair? That they were overreacting, because it will be years yet before you're ready for marriage? Perhaps the following paragraphs will help you appreciate what they had in mind.

Surely there is nothing immoral in a Jew's dating a non-Jew. Yet it can be very dangerous. No one decides in advance when or with whom to fall in love. The more you grow accustomed to dating non-Jews, the greater the probability of your falling in love with and wanting to marry one. I have known several couples who established a romantic relationship in high school that persisted through the years to the point of marriage.

It is likely that Jews who establish in high school a general pattern of dating non-Jews will continue that pattern in college. In this connection it would be wise for young people who apparently prefer non-Jews to Jews for dating to ask themselves why. Is it in rebellion against their parents? In resentment of being Jewish? In either case the motive is not a healthy one, and the prognosis for a good marriage is poor.

*L*IFE OR DEATH FOR JUDAISM? Two reasons above all others account for the strong opposition of most Jewish leaders to intermarriage. First is the ominous threat to Jewish survival. Our Jewish proportion of the total United States population has been steadily declining. In 1937 we were 3.7 percent of the total, in 1963 only 2.9 percent of the total. If present trends continue, it has been estimated that by the year 2000 no more than 1.6 percent of the population will be Jews. Intermarriage is beyond doubt a major factor accounting for this rapid decline. Rabbi David Einhorn, one of the early leaders of American Reform Judaism, was more prophetic than he himself may have thought when nearly a century ago he wrote: "Intermarriage drives a nail in the coffin of Judaism." His dire prediction is confirmed by the estimate of experts that in the United States today as many as 70 percent of the children born to intermarried couples end up with no Jewish identity at all.

No one who is convinced that the survival of Judaism and the Jewish people is important, not only for themselves but also for the further enrichment of civilization, can treat such evidence lightly.

*H*EAVY BURDEN Another reason for opposing inter-marriage is the decreased probability of happiness and success. Shared religious experience can be one of the strongest positive factors producing marital happiness. In intermarriage this possibility becomes instead destructive. This does not mean that every mixed marriage is doomed, or that every marriage within a given religious group is guaranteed to succeed. What it does mean is that, in the often delicate balance determining the pluses or minuses of each marriage, mixed religious backgrounds constitute a serious hazard.

The facts confirm this conclusion. The divorce rate is three to four times higher among mixed-marriage couples than among others. A study published a few years ago by the American Youth Commission showed the number of young people in several categories who came from broken homes:

Both parents Jewish	4.6% from broken homes
Both parents Catholic	6.4% from broken homes
Both parents Protestant	6.8% from broken homes
Parents from mixed religions	15.2% from broken homes
Parents with no religion	16.7% from broken homes

This is not difficult to understand. We must remember—regarding Judaism perhaps even more than other religions—that religion is more than just theological belief. It also involves attitudes toward the meaning of life, frames of reference on sex, patterns of family behavior, idioms and idiosyncrasies of language, matters of food and holiday observance, and similar items. A Jew who is accustomed to celebrating Chanukah and Passover would find it extremely difficult to observe Christmas and Easter instead. A Christian who had always taken Communion in church might miss this tradition painfully. There are many subtle yet vital patterns of life—no less imperative in that they may be taken for granted—whose absence or disruption can pose serious threats to personal security.

There is a maximum threshold of strain any husband and wife can tolerate, a point beyond which their marriage will fail. Mixed religious background constitutes one of the heaviest burdens any couple can bear. Those who blithely dismiss the experience of others, who marry out of a naive confidence that they will surely succeed where so many others have failed, do themselves a menacing disservice.

INNOCENT VICTIMS Disagreements about child-rearing practices are often the major cause of failed intermarriages, and the children of these marriages are the chief victims. Neat intellectual "solutions" agreed upon in advance often fail to stand up before the stubborn realities of life. Even two of the most sensitive and perceptive young people romantically involved with each other cannot possibly realize what it would be like one day to behold their own precious child, fruit of their bodies and their love. To agree in advance that a child will be reared in no religious tradition or in that of one's mate may seem like such a simple thing. But, when the child actually snuggles in your arms, suddenly what seemed so simple can become complicated and snarled. Circumcision, Bar or Bat Mitzvah, and Confirmation for the Jew—Baptism and Communion for the Christian—there is no way to prepare ahead of time for what these moments can mean later.

The testimony of Rachel Cowan is especially instructive here. She became a Jew-by-Choice after marrying her late husband, then felt so enamored of Judaism that she was ordained a Reform rabbi. Listen to what she says about intermarried couples:

Just as many Jews who marry Gentiles are often surprised to discover that they feel an inexplicably powerful commitment to Jewish survival, so many Christians who wed Jews come to the sudden, unexpected realization that they care more than they had thought about Jesus, about the Church, about the meaning of Christmas and Easter.

Often these religious and cultural feelings are suppressed when a Jewish-Christian couple falls in love. They come to the surface as marriage approaches or when children are born. We call these feelings time bombs in an interfaith relationship. . . .

If you are the child of an interfaith couple (remember: if conversion has taken place, the match is no longer considered a case of mixed marriage), you may already know from personal experience the significance of Rachel Cowan's words. Yet there is something else you must know: The very facts that you are studying in a Jewish school and that your parents are members of a temple show that one of the major objections to mixed marriage doesn't apply in your case. There would seem to be no danger that Judaism will become extinct in your family.

Does the second chief argument against intermarriage apply to you? Are your parents happily, successfully married? Has the difference in their religious background been troubling for them?

You are better qualified than I to answer these questions, probably better than anyone else on earth. You should also be aware that–regardless of whether your originally Christian parent did or did not become Jewish–in Reform Judaism so long as you have received a Jewish education and lived as a Jew, you are fully accepted by your rabbi, your teachers, and your classmates as a Jew.

So, we end this part of our discussion where we began. The next time your parents criticize you for wanting to date a non-Jew, you may be able to understand better than before the worries that underlie their concern.

*W*HAT DO YOU THINK? Neither Dick nor Norma has ever been particularly religious. He hasn't seen the inside of a church for years nor she a synagogue. They were certain, therefore, that their differing religions would not be an issue in their marriage.

Dick began to change after their first son was born. At first the change was subtle. He would occasionally attend church services on a Sunday morning without mentioning it to Norma. Soon he went to church every week. Then he enrolled in a Monday night Bible class and began to bring missionary tracts home.

Norma resented this, feeling it violated their premarital agreement to remain religiously neutral. She wasn't sure whether it was religious conviction that moved her or just a desire for revenge, but she began to observe a few Jewish rituals in their home. Their son was sent to Hebrew school as soon as he was old enough.

It was her plans for a Bar Mitzvah that really brought things to a head. She insisted on it. Dick threatened he wouldn't attend if it were held, and the boy felt trapped between warring parents. At this point their son developed so many symptoms of tension that he was referred by his school for psychiatric help.

Does this sound to you like a real or a manufactured story? What solutions can you suggest? Should there be a Bar Mitzvah? Could both parents be satisfied by celebrating a Bar Mitzvah in a synagogue as well as Confirmation in Dick's church? What can we learn from this case?

*S*HALOM You are not making your choice of a mate now. But you are shaping your personality and values; you are acquiring new knowledge and forming new attitudes; you are making other important decisions every day, all of which will eventually add up to your choice of a mate when the proper time comes. There is always a strong bond between present and future. What you do today helps determine what you will be and do tomorrow. Each important decision you make is like another number placed in a long column for addition. You have considerable freedom to choose what each number is to be, but once the numbers have been listed, once the choices made, what you are at any given moment is their sum total. No number can be erased. They can be counteracted by later subtractions, but it is very much harder to do this than to insert the correct number in the first place. In this sense your attitudes and conduct now have much to do with your choice of a spouse in the future.

That choice will require the keenest intelligence, the sharpest sensitivity, the most mature balance, you possess. And all these invaluable traits can be enhanced by the insights of Judaism and of science. My highest hope in these chapters has been to supply you with at least the beginning of such skills. May you, too, one day enjoy a marriage filled with richness, fulfillment and love.

NOTES
DATE OR MATE?
 1. E. W. Burgess and L. S. Cottrell, *Predicting Success or Failure in Mariage* (Englewood Cliffs, N.J.: Prentice-Hall, 1939), p. 62.
 2. S. Gordon and C. Snyder, *Personal Issues in Human Sexuality* (Boston: Allyn & Bacon, 1986), pp. 10ff.